WILLIAM AVERY
'BILLY' BISHOP

DAVID BAKER

· OUTLINE PRESS ·

AN OUTLINE PRESS BOOK

Copyright © DAVID BAKER 1990
First published in Great Britain in 1990 by
Outline Press (Book Publishers) Limited
115J Cleveland Street
London W1P 5PN
ISBN 1.871547.07.5

A CIP catalogue record for this book is
available from the British Library.

This book was designed and produced by
THE OUTLINE PRESS

Typesetting by Midford Typesetting Ltd.

Printed and bound by Grafoimpex, Zagreb, Yugoslavia.

DESIGN	*Nigel Osborne*
EDITOR	*Sarah Baker*
ARTWORK	*Mike Roffe*
PHOTOGRAPHY	*Matthew Chattle*

Contents

INTRODUCTION *William Avery 'Billy' Bishop*   **4-5**

CHAPTER ONE *Boldly to the Foe*   **6-16**

CHAPTER TWO *A War With Choices*   **17-31**

CHAPTER THREE *Wings of Victory*   **32-55**

CHAPTER FOUR *Aces High*   **56-90**

CHAPTER FIVE *An Ace Supreme*   **91-114**

CHAPTER SIX *Technical Details*   **115-127**

INTRODUCTION *William Avery 'Billy' Bishop*

This is the second book in the Famous Flyers series and tells the story of Canada's top scoring fighter pilot of World War I. In the ranks of Allied air aces, Billy Bishop officially stands third, behind Frenchman Rene Fonck, with 75 victories, and Irishman Mick Mannock, credited with 73 victories. As it is, he was the highest scoring Canadian and with 79 'unofficial' victories to his credit he may have been second only to the leading ace of that war, Manfred Freiherr von Richthofen.

But precise and accurate victory logs are impossible to find and there is speculation about the exact number of victories he actually achieved. Sadly, Billy Bishop died in 1956 at the comparatively young age of 62 and we are unable to seek and obtain clarification for many fights where, apart from the victim, he was the only participant.

It is quite possible that information contained in this book will be updated as further research adds to the body of knowledge about the man and his activities. The author welcomes correspondence from readers who can add to the story and, if the information is authenticated, future editions will be revised to carry these changes and amendments.

Many people have helped in the preparation of this book. The author and his publishers would like to thank Timothy Graves for providing much useful information, including the combat reports and some of the pictures. Without his help and valuable contributions it would not be as complete as it is. Thanks for quotations are due to Bailey Bros. & Swinfen who in 1975 published Billy Bishop's book Winged Warfare. Acknowledgement for some historical aspects of No. 60 Squadron go to Joe Warne who has published a detailed analysis of that unit's operations in the journal of the Cross & Cockade society.

Readers who wish to learn more about this exciting period of aviation history are heartily encouraged to contact Cross & Cockade International via the Membership Secretary, Mrs Christine A. Leaman, Cragg Cottage, The Cragg, Bramham, Wetherby, West Yorkshire LS23 6QB, England. Cross & Cockade publish a quarterly journal which contains useful information on aviation throughout the period 1914-1918. Additional information on World War I aircraft and on models of that period can be found in the highly recommended bi-monthly publication, Windsock International, from Albatros Publications Ltd, 10 Long View, Berkhampstead, Herts HP4 1BY, England.

Special thanks must go to the Royal Air Force Museum at Hendon England, and to the Imperial War Museum.
Thanks are also due to Mike Roffe for his special skills in providing all the original artwork in this book and to Sarah, my wife, editor and constant help in guiding the way this book was finally written. From them both, and my publishers Nigel Osborne and Peter Owen, I absolve all responsibility for any errors this book may inadvertently contain.

"I have not to this day fully analysed my feelings in those moments of my first victory. I don't think I fully realised what it all meant." William Avery Bishop

CHAPTER ONE *Boldly to the Foe*

The air war of early summer 1917 was taking a grim turn for the worse. In what became known throughout the Royal Flying Corps as 'Bloody April', British airmen had suffered during the spring one of their worst batterings since air combat began in August 1914. Marshalled to support the British First and Third Armies, the Royal Flying Corps had put up 25 squadrons with 365 aircraft to help General Sir Douglas Haig with his massive push at the Battle of Arras. It was planned in conjunction with a strategic assault on the Aisne by the brilliant French General Robert Nivelle which was to have broken the German grip and transformed stagnant trench warfare into a running fight to the finish.

For thirty-two months the armed forces of Germany, France, Belgium and Great Britain, supported by large contingents from foreign territories, fought to the death over trenches and stinking shell holes along a line stretching 400 miles from the English Channel to the Swiss border west of Basel. Seduced by the promise of a final coup de grace to an unhappy, unending war that was already taking its toll of politicians, British and French optimism for early success clouded logic.

In Britain, Lloyd George had replaced Asquith as Prime Minister when the latter drowned en route to Russia after his ship, the *Hampshire*, hit a German mine. Lloyd George wanted a victory and was persuaded by Nivelle that a human wave rising in assault upon the German lines could bring the 'Boche' to their knees. Nivelle had risen to favour at the end of 1916 and replaced General Joffre as the French Commander-in-Chief. His brilliant use of heavy artillery in counter attacks at Verdun led politicans to trust him when they should have sought caution.

A year before, the Somme had given the war its bloodiest day, the British alone sustaining 60,000 casualties. When it came during April, the Chemin des Dames Offensive (so called after a small road across the River Aisne) turned the Champagne area north of Reims into a veritable bloodbath. About 40,000 men lost their lives on the first day. Up and down the Western Front more than 6.4 million soldiers faced each other - 16,000 every mile. About 3.9 million of them were French, British and Belgian. On the Champagne sector the offensive raged on only because Nivelle did not have the courage to admit he had been wrong.

Wave after wave of infantry hurled themselves upon the German positions and despite declaring he would win the war in 24 hours it was ten days before Nivelle admitted defeat. In that time nearly 300,000 Frenchmen had been slaughtered, more than a thousand each hour without respite for ten long days. The losses on the Aisne almost broke the French forces. More than half the divisions revolted, the troops turning on their officers and deserting their posts. Nivelle went, Marshal Petain replaced him, and order was restored for more battles on other days. It was a prelude to Passchendaele where grand strategies would again come to nothing after a further 500,000 men had been killed, maimed or wounded; 40,000 were sucked into the mud and never found.

It was typical of the attitude of these comrades of mine that when a man had been in an exceedingly tight corner and had managed to squeeze out of it, it was later related as a very amusing, not as a very terrible, incident, and as the narrator would tell his story the others would shriek with laughter at the tale of how nearly he had been hit and how 'scared' he had been. It was such a wonderful way to take life that, upon looking back at it, I feel that nothing the future can ever hold for me can excel those wonderful days. Face to face with death every day, but always with the best of comrades and the most tried of friends, it has left a wonderful memory with me.

Such was the background to events that gave Canada's greatest fighting airman of World War I the highest military medal bestowed by Britain: the Victoria Cross. The recipient was Capt. William Avery Bishop, better known as Billy Bishop, of No. 60 Sqdn, RFC. The event for which he was to be awarded the V.C. occurred during the artillery bombardment which preceded the Battle of Messines. It took place on June 2, 1917, between the Aisne and Arras offensives which ended in late April and the Battle for Passchendaele which would begin at the end of July.

Although numerically overwhelmed, the superior performance of German Albatros scout aircraft allowed them to wreak havoc on pusher aircraft like the D.H.2 and the F.E.2. With a forward firing gun and an engine behind, the latter were no real match for the Albatros' classic fighter design employing an in-line engine with twin, fixed, forward-firing machine guns. A year earlier, the Royal Flying Corps had emerged from a period

One of the distinguished German flying squadrons opposite us was under command of the famous Captain Baron von Richthofen. One day I had the distinction of engaging in three fights in half an hour with pilots from this squadron. Their machines were painted a brilliant scarlet from nose to tail - immense red birds, they were, with the graceful wings of the type, Albatros scouts. They were all single-seaters, and were flown by pilots of undeniable skill. There was quite a little spirit of sportsmanship in this squadron, too. The red German machines had two machine guns in fixed positions firing straight ahead, both being operated from the same control.

Below
German Fokker Dr.I fighters stand ready at an airfield in France. Although not common practice, seeking the enemy at his base was an effective way of destroying German aircraft.

identified colloquially as the 'Fokker scourge' where single-seat Fokker monoplanes married a synchronised machine gun to a small airframe of relative agility and crisp performance.

Fokker monoplanes had been the first operational fighters designed solely for the purpose of shooting down enemy aircraft and stimulated a response from the Allies which established the fighter as a tactical weapon in its own right. Now, having handed the baton of superior fighter design to the Albatros Flugzeugwerke, Germany would be stuck with biplanes from this bureau for the rest of the war. But in June 1917, the definitive Albatros D.V was making its appearance. Billy Bishop would shoot down more Albatros fighters than any other type of aircraft.

Just emerging too was the single-seat British S.E.5, designed and developed by the Royal Aircraft Factory at Farnborough, Hampshire, and the two-seat Bristol F.2A. But the S.E.5 was not available in sufficient numbers, nor were its teething troubles properly ironed out to give leading exponents the confidence to throw it heartily into combat. Yet the S.E.5, and its modified variant the S.E.5a, would quickly develop into an effective fighting machine. Billy Bishop would use its assets well when he began flying this type exclusively from the end of July 1917

In the preceding month, however, Bishop had the use of a Nieuport scout, a type he had flown since scoring his first combat victory less than three months before. Now, with 28 victories officially credited to him, Billy Bishop was about to embark upon the single most talked about event in squadron messes along the Western Front that June, in an aircraft that for two years had excelled itself against the enemy.

The single-seat Nieuport 10 first appeared in mid-1915 and quickly adopted the name Bebe (Baby). Powered by a 80 hp Gnome rotary, its performance was improved when fitted with a 110 hp Le Rhone and it became the Type 16. The Nieuport 17 was bigger, much stronger, and could take the 130 hp Clerget rotary engine. On all Nieuport scouts the bottom wing had a slightly narrower span than the top wing but much reduced chord. They were called sesquiplanes, a term derived from the Latin word sesqui, meaning one and one-half, since the smaller bottom wing only seemed to do half the work of the top wing!

Above
Diminutive, agile and fast, the Nieuport 17 was the perfect mount for Billy Bishop as he sought out the enemy in the skies above the Western Front.

The French Nieuport sesquiplane scouts arrived in time to oust the Fokker monoplanes along with the British designed D.H.2 in early 1916. Not before Albatros introduced the D.I in late 1916 did the Germans have a machine that could tackle the diminutive but powerful little biplane. Yet whereas the D.H.2 was outclassed by early 1917 the Nieuport series of scouts developed into a line of useful Allied fighting aeroplanes employed on front-line duty to the end of the war.

Equipped with a single 0.303 inch Lewis machine gun attached to a Foster mounting (named after Sgt. Foster of No. 11 Sqdn, RFC) on the upper centre section of the top wing, the Nieuport 17 could reach 10,000 feet in nine minutes, almost six minutes faster than the Albatros D.V. The RFC made good use of this valuable asset and one of the greatest exponents of it was the British pilot, Albert Ball, whose remarkable success with the little sesquiplane turned him into a role idol for Billy Bishop.

When flying alone, on a day off or something like that, I took queer chances, it is true, but flying with the patrol often let opportunities slip by because they were not quite good enough; but when the right ones came, we were quick to seize them and were nearly always successful.
I had learned that the most important thing in fighting was the shooting, next the various tactics in coming into the fight, and last of all flying ability itself. The shooting, as I have said before, I practised constantly and became more and more expert at it, with the result that finally I had great confidence in myself, and knew for a certainty that if I could get in a shot from one or two of my favourite positions, I would be successful in downing my opponent.

Intent upon reaching and exceeding Ball's incredible score of 44 confirmed victories in eleven months, Bishop met Ball on May 5. Ball came over from No. 56 Sqdn, RFC, to visit No. 60 Sqdn and talked with Bishop about the two of them conducting a surprise dawn strike on a German airfield. A furious and very courageous fighter who knew no fear and gave no quarter, Albert Ball was a kindred spirit for the Canadian. He saw in Bishop a like-minded fighting man and wanted to seize the opportunity provided by a new policy at RFC Headquarters: to use the fighting scout as a ground attack plane.

Exploited informally in this role as early as mid-1916, improved performance and load carrying capacity of aircraft a year later made that application potentially even more attractive as a formally planned activity. Lt. Col. Wilfred R. Freeman developed the concept of artillery being used to suppress anti-aircraft fire while ground attack planes strafed and bombed the trenches from a mere 50 feet or so. Only three days before Ball met Bishop to plan the daring airfield attack, No. 40 Sqdn, RFC, demonstrated the Freeman doctrine by sending six Nieuports across the lines at zero height to attack a line of observation balloons. Four were shot down.

Two days after Bishop and Ball generally agreed upon a surprise attack, the 20 year old fighting airman from Nottingham, England, was killed when his aircraft plummeted to earth through cloud. He was never seen again. But Bishop, his imagination fired by the daring-do of the young Englishman, was not ready to abandon the idea so firmly entrenched just days before. He was resolved to carry out the raid - on his own if necessary. The opportunity came within a few weeks and Bishop decided on June 1 that the following morning he would go in search of a vulnerable German airfield.

"I knew I would strike the Huns by surprise and, considering that, I decided the risk was not nearly as great as it seemed, and that I might be able to get four or five more machines to my credit in one great swoop," Bishop wrote late in 1917. *"At 3 o'clock I was called and got up. It was pitch-black. I dressed and went in to tell my friends that I was off. They were not entirely in favour of the expedition, and said so again. Notwithstanding this, I went on to the aerodrome and got away as the first streaks of dawn were showing in the upper sky."*

Billy Bishop took off in a Nieuport Type 17 with serial number B1566, an aircraft he had flown many times before. In this, he had scored eighteen victories and shared one other with a Lt. William Fry, also from No. 60 Sqdn. *"I flew straight across the lines toward the aerodrome I had planned to attack, and coming down low, decided to carry out my plan and stir them up with a burst of machine gun fire into their hangar sheds. But on reaching the place, I saw there was nothing on the ground. In the meantime for something to do I flew along low over the country in the hope of coming on some camp or ground troops so as to scatter them.*

"I felt that the danger was nil, as most of the crews of the guns which ordinarily would fire at me would still be asleep, and I might as well give any Huns I could find a good fright. I was in rather a bad temper at having my carefully laid plan fall through so quickly, and nothing would have pleased me better than to have run across a group of fat Huns drilling in a field, or something of that sort. However, nothing appeared and I was just thinking of turning and going home, or of climbing up to see if there were some Huns in the upper sky, when ahead, and slightly to one side of me, I saw the sheds of another aerodrome.

"I at once decided that here was my chance, although it was not a very favourable one, as the aerodrome was pretty far back from the lines. To make good my escape would not be as easy as I had hoped. Furthermore I was not even certain where I was and that was my greatest worry as I was a bit afraid that if I had any bad fights I might have trouble in finding my way back. Scurrying along close to the ground, zigzagging here and there, one's sense of direction becomes slightly vague. Another half-minute and I was over the aerodrome, about 300 feet up.

"On the ground were seven German machines, and in my first glance I saw that some of them actually had their engines

running. Mechanics were standing around in groups. Then I saw a thing that surprised me - six of the machines were single-seaters and one a two-seater. I pointed my nose towards the ground and opened fire with my gun, scattering bullets all around the machines and coming down to 50 feet in so doing. I do not know how many men I hit, or what damage was done, except that one man, at least, fell and several others ran to pick him up. Then clearing off to one side, I watched the fun.

'' I had forgotten by this time that they would of course have machine guns on the aerodrome, and as I was laughing to myself as they tore around in every direction on the ground, I heard the familiar rattle of the quick-firers on me. I did not dare go too far away, however, as then I would not be able to catch the machines as they left the ground, so turning quickly and twisting about, I did my best to evade the fire from the ground. Looking at my planes I saw that the guns were doing pretty good shooting.

'' Then one machine began to taxi off down the aerodrome. It increased its speed quickly and I immediately tore down after it. I managed to close on its tail, when it was just above the ground and opened fire from dead behind it. There was no chance of missing and I was as cool as could be. Just fifteen rounds and it side-slipped to one side, then crashed on the aerodrome underneath. I was now keyed up to the fight, and turning quickly, saw another machine just off the ground. Taking careful aim at it, I fired from longer range than before, as I did not want to waste the time of going up close.

'' For one awful moment I saw my bullets missing, and aimed still more carefully, all the time striving to get nearer. The Hun saw I was catching him up, and pushed his nose down; then, gazing over his shoulder at the moment I was firing, he crashed into some trees near the aerodrome. I think I hit him just before he came to the trees, as my tracers were going in an accurate line. I again turned towards the aerodrome. This time my heart sank, bcause two machines were taking off at the same time, and in slightly different directions.

'' It was the one thing I had dreaded. There was not much wind, and it was possible for them to do this. I had made up my mind, before, that if they attempted to do this I would immediately make good my escape, but I had counted on being higher. However, true to my intention, I began to climb. One of the enemy luckily climbed away at some distance, while the other made straight for me. At 1,000 feet, and only a few hundred yards from the aerodrome, I saw that he was catching me, so turned on him and opened fire.

'' These were wonderfully interesting days to me. Late the next afternoon I had the good fortune to be a spectator of the greatest fight in the air I have ever seen. Thrilling fights are often witnessed from the ground, but more of them take place at heights so misty that ground observers know nothing of them, unless one or more of the combatants should come tumbling down in a crash. More than often fights in the air would go unobserved if it were not for the 'Archie' shells breaking in the sky. These shells play about friend and foe alike, but when you are really intent upon an air duel the 'Archies' make no impression upon you whatever. **''**

Far left
German Army Air Service Jagdstaffeln sometimes operated out of tents, achieving mobility and flexible operations.

It used to amuse and amaze me to think, on days like this, of the marvels that modern flying had accomplished. Our machines were not only called upon to fly faster by far than the swiftest birds, but to do 'stunts' that no bird ever thought of. Whoever heard of a bird flying upside-down? Yet there were plenty of our pilots who rather delighted in doing this. There are trick flyers just as there are trick bicyclists and trick riders in the circus. I belonged to the steady flyers' class, but some day soon I am really going to learn to fly, to do aerial acrobatics, and everything.

We made about two circuits around each other, neither getting a very good shot, but in the end I managed to get in a short burst of fire, and his machine went crashing to the ground, where it lay in a field, a few hundred yards from the aerodrome. The fourth machine then came up, and I opened fire on him. I was now greatly worried as to how I was to get away, as I was using up all my ammunition, and there seemed to be no end to the number of machines coming up. I was afraid that other machines from other aerodromes would also come in answer to telephone calls, and wanted to get away as quickly as I could.

But there was no chance of running from this man - he had me cold - so I turned at him savagely, and in the course of the fight, emptied my last drum at him. Luckily, at the moment I finished my ammunition, he also seemed to have had enough of it, as he turned away. I seized my opportunity, climbed away, and started for home. To my dismay I discovered four enemy scouts above me. I was terrified that they would see me, so flew directly underneath them for some time - almost a mile, I should think - going directly south.

Then, deciding that I must do something, I took the bit between my teeth and slipped away. They did not attempt to attack me at all, so I am not sure whether they even saw me or not. I now headed in the approximate direction of our lines, and flew in rather a dazed state toward them. I had not had any breakfast, and was feeling very queer at my stomach. The excitement, and the reaction afterward had been a bit too much, as well as the cold morning air. It seemed once or twice that my head was going around and around, and that something must happen.

For the only moment in my life it entered my thoughts that I might lose my senses in a moment, and go insane. It was a horrible feeling, and I also had the terrible sensation that I would suffer from nausea at any minute. I was not at all sure where I was, and furthermore did not care. The thrills and exultation I had first felt had all died away, and nothing seemed to matter but this awful dizziness and the desire to get home and on the ground.

By the time I reached the aerodrome, however, I felt much better, and flew over our still sleeping huts, firing off my signal lights frantically to show them I had certainly had some success. I landed, and my sergeant immediately rushed and asked how many I had bagged. When I told him three, he was greatly pleased, and yelled it back to the mechanics who were waiting by the shed. Then as I crawled out of my machine, I heard the remarks of the mechanics around me. They were looking it over.

Everywhere it was shot about, bullet holes being in almost every part of it, although none, luckily, within two feet of where I sat. Parts of the machine were so badly damaged as to take a lot of repairing. "

What the mechanics found was that the lower wing of the silver doped Nieuport had been shot away in two places and that the aircraft had a total of seventeen bullet holes. This is not excessive for the amount of action seen by Bishop that morning. Twelve bullet holes were grouped closely together close to where Bishop's head would have rested against the shallow faired-in head rest on top of the fuselage. Later that day, Bishop filed a customary combat report and modestly described one of the most outstanding actions of the first war in the air:

Combats in the Air

Squadron: 60
Type and No. of Aeroplane: Nieuport Sct. B1566
Armament: 1 Lewis Gun
Pilot: Capt W. A. Bishop D.S.O. MC.
Observer: None
Locality: Either Esnes aerodrome or Awoignt.
Remarks on Hostile Machine:- Albatros scouts

Date: June 2nd 1917
Time: 4.23 - 5 a.m.
Duty: H.A.
Height: 50-7,000 ft

I fired on 7 machines on the aerodrome, some of which had their engines running. One of them took off and I fired 15 rounds at him from close range 60 feet up and he crashed. A second one taking off, I opened fire and fired 30 rounds at 150 yards range, he crashed into a tree. Two more were then taking off together. I climbed and engaged one at 1,000 feet, finishing my drum, and he crashed 300 yards from the aerodrome. I changed drums and climbed E(ast). A fourth H.A. came after me and I fired one whole drum into him. He flew away and I then flew 1,000 feet under four scouts at 5,000 feet for one mile and turned W(est) climbing. The aerodrome was armed with one or more machine guns. Machines on the ground were 6 scouts (Albatros Type I or II) and one two-seater.

(Sgd) W. A. Bishop Capt.

"It was apparent to us by this time that the Germans were bringing their best pilots opposite the British front to meet the determined offensive we had been carrying on since April 1st. Most of the machines we met were handled in a manner far above the German average. Each night our pilots brought in exciting stories of the the chase. Although they were a higher class of fighting men than we had hitherto flown against, the Germans still showed a reluctance to attack unless they outnumbered us by at least three to one. One lone German was induced to take a fatal chance against a British scout formation. By clever manoeuvring, at which the hostile airman was also quite adept, we managed to entice him to attack one of our machines from behind. As he did so, a second British machine dived at him and down he went, one of his wings breaking off as he fell."

Identification of the Albatros type was relatively easy even at a distance and under such stressful combat conditions as those that prevailed during the dawn attack. The Albatros D.I and D.II had equal span, equal chord wings with single interplane struts fore and aft on either side. All subsequent Albatros scouts had 'V'shaped interplane struts connecting the sesquiplane wing design which had itself been inspired by the apparent success of the Nieuport. The earlier Albatros scouts were going out of service as the D.III and the D.V were reaching German Jagdstaffeln in increasing numbers. In June, there were little more than a hundred in operational service.

Additional detail on the events of June 2, 1917, came from Lt. William Fry who shared an adjacent room to Bishop in the same Nissen hut at No. 60 Sqdn. Lt. Fry was deputy to Bishop as leader of C Flight and came to know him well. The two flew together on several occasions and Bishop shared a victory with Fry when they shot down a two-seater. Lt. Fry was with Bishop the evening before his dawn raid:

"The night before, we were enjoying one of our noisy parties in the mess - probably celebrating a decoration awarded to someone. Bishop approached me during the evening and said something about shooting up an enemy aerodrome early next morning and would I care to go with him. I did not take much notice, was non-committal, and soon afterwards went to bed.

"Early the following morning, before light, he came into my room and asked if I were going with him. I had a headache from the night's party and answered that I was not for it, turned over and went to sleep again. It should be explained that it was an entirely voluntary effort and there was no question of him having been detailed for the job. Later, an hour or so after dawn, Bishop came into my room in an excited state and told me how he had shot up a German aerodrome and also destroyed several aircraft which had come up to attack him.

"He said he had managed to cross the line further south in the French sector, despite being followed and attacked all the way, had landed in a field behind the French lines to find out where he was, and having got his bearings from some French worker on the land, flew back home. He arrived back without his machine gun, having undone the screw-up release on the securing collar and thrown the gun overboard after he had let it down on its quadrant to put on a fresh ammunition drum while being attacked on the way home.

"At that point he had found himself unable to get the new drum on or the gun back in the firing position. At breakfast there was a buzz of talk in the mess. On going over to the flight hangar I saw Bishop's machine was the centre of attraction. I remember clearly seeing a group of five bullet holes in the rear half of the tailplane, the elevator, within a circle of not more than six inches diameter at the most. Whatever machine was on his tail must have been very close indeed to achieve this group."

After breakfast, when he had had time to recover, the C.O. obtained details from him in some sequence and his combat report was made out. The Commanding Officer of No. 60 Sqdn, RFC, Maj. A. J. L. Scott, made out a special confidential report to Headquarters, 13th Wing, RFC, on what he termed "an extremely brilliant individual attack on a German aerodrome near Cambrai." This daring act of bravery and skill, tinged with more than a little luck, was quickly brought to the notice of General Haig and, as Lt. Fry relates, to a direct means by which a recommendation for the Victoria Cross could be made.

"In a village a few miles away was Third Army Advanced Headquarters. Our C.O., Major Scott, had access to General Allenby, commanding Third Army, through his friend Lord Dalmeny who was Allenby's (Assistant) Military Secretary. Major Scott telephoned him about Bishop's exploit and was invited to take him over to see the Army Commander who wanted to hear his story at first hand. For some reason, probably just for the outing, I was taken too, and after Bishop had told his story to the Army Commander we had luncheon in one of the Headquarters messes." Billy Bishop was awarded the Victoria Cross on August 11, 1917, giving him Britain's highest military award for bravery.

CHAPTER TWO *A War With Choices*

Until the 20th century, citizens mustered to the nation's defence had little option but to join the army or the navy. It was not much of an option. Soldiers had the choice of carrying a rifle or a musket into battle facing artillery or cannon, joining the cavalry with added responsibilities for the welfare of horse as well as mind and body, or adding to the seemingly endless army of supernumeries such as stores clerks, supply personnel, cooks and bottle washers. Moreover, the choices were usually made by someone else.

With the iron warship, steam engines and big guns operated by large numbers of men in hot, cramped conditions, a sailor's life was equally unpleasant. For soldiers at least, war on the Western Front was the epitome of a ghoulish nightmare and many sought ways to escape into less uncomfortable jobs. It was to escape the drudgery and discomfort of army life that William Avery Bishop applied in July 1915, to join the Royal Flying Corps as an observer. It was the turning point in his life and as events would prove, a short route to fame. For Billy Bishop, it would seem that life held an uncertain future until the day he traded mud and boredom for a chance to fly and fight in the air. After all, he had come a long way to get to grips with the 'Boche' and do his bit for King and country.

Born on February 8, 1894, to William and Margaret Bishop, Billy was the eldest of three sons. County registrar and a strict Liberal, his father held a generally conservative attitude to life and refrained from fashionable changes or fickle trends in popular opinion. This meant that William required Billy to be dressed by his mother in the form of a young version of himself and the boy quickly fell foul of ribald jest when he was sent to school wearing a grey suit with collar and tie, and very scrubbed hands and face.

Probably for this reason, and because Billy was less gregarious than fellow school mates, the boy quickly developed a fractious attitude to criticism. Ever ready with his fists to put right an argument that went against him, Billy stood up for himself and gained ground, gathering respect from his junior peers. He soon found he had a natural talent for sports. His interests lay in shooting, riding, swimming and generally showing the world at large that although it considered him an indifferent outsider he could, on his own terms, still hold his own.

Born and raised in Owen Sound, Ontario, Billy Bishop entered the Royal Military College at Kingston, Ontario, during August 1911. He was 17 years old and determined to succeed, cramming hard for the entrance exam that Billy, not an academic lad by nature, found hard. Thanks largely to his tutors' help, he passed the entrance examination and went to school on the banks of the St. Lawrence. The young trainee officer found life hard on two counts. He was expected to do well at team sports and apply himself strenuously to academic studies and he was expected to respect a military code of orders without question.

It was the mud, I think, that made me take to flying. I had fully expected that going into battle would mean for me the saddle of a galloping charger, instead of the snug little cockpit of a modern aeroplane. The mud, on a certain day in July 1915, changed my whole career in the war. We were in England. I had gone over as an officer of the Mississauga Horse, of Toronto, a cavalry detachment of the Second Canadian Division. It had rained for days in torrents, and there was still a drizzle coming down as I set out for a tour of the horse-lines.
Ordinary mud is bad enough, when you have to make your home in it, but the particular brand of mud that infests a cavalry camp has a meanness all its own. Everything was dank, and slimy, and boggy. I had succeeded in getting myself mired to the knees when suddenly, from somewhere out of the storm, appeared a trim little aeroplane.

The individualistic approach to life already nurtured by Billy Bishop ran counter to this and he found life very hard during his first year at college. But he worked to constrain himself within the rigid institutional framework of the regime and although infringing the rules on numerous occasions he was given a second chance, entering his second year on the grounds that he stay at college longer to make up for his wasted first year. The second year was better for Bishop and he achieved good pass marks in the summer examinations.

The third year brought a serious condemnation from the college commandant when Bishop was caught using crib sheets for the May 1914 exams. It was petty, youthful cheating but at the Royal Military College it was taken seriously indeed. The young Bishop faced the very real threat of being dismissed from the college but a final decision was deferred until the end of the summer. By that time war clouds gathering in Europe brought grave concern to thinking Canadians. Links through Empire were strong and Britain might have to go to war; might have to fight the central European powers and call upon her colonial manpower to fill the breach.

Every able bodied man would be needed and Billy Bishop suddenly found himself commissioned into the Mississauga Horse of Toronto, a cavalry detachment with the 2nd Canadian Division. Not for long, however. A bout of pneumonia kept him behind in a hospital bed when his unit left for England with the Canadian Expeditionary Force so Billy was assigned to the 14th Battalion, Canadian Mounted Rifles, then forming in London, Ontario.

For several months he waited with his unit as preparations for embarkation were completed. About to leave Canada for the first time and soon to fight a war which had the proud old countries of Europe pitched in bloody conflict, Billy proposed to his long time girl friend Margaret Burden and was accepted. Before him lay a two week boat trip across the North Atlantic where German U-boats lurked in wait for merchant ships. Berthed at Montreal, the requisitioned cattleship *Caledonia* was to carry the 14th across to England along with horses and supplies that dramatically overloaded the creaking ship. With stormy weather, heaving seas and ill horses, the flower of Canadian youth began their journey to war. On June 23, 1915, the *Caledonia* mercifully slipped into Plymouth harbour, safe from German submarines and the unpleasant effects of sea-sick horses. By this time the pattern of the war in Europe had become all too clear, although there was little sign of it in

" It landed hesitatingly in a nearby field as if scorning to brush its wings against so sordid a landscape; then away again up into the clean grey mists.
How long I stood there gazing into the distance I do not know, but when I turned to slog my way back through the mud my mind was made up. I knew there was only one place to be on such a day - up above the clouds and in the summer sunshine. I was going into the battle that way. I was going to meet the enemy in the air.
I had never given much thought to being a soldier, even after my parents had sent me to the Royal Military College at Kingston, when I was seventeen years of age. I will say for my parents that they had not thought much of me as a professional soldier either. But they did think, for some reason or other, that a little military discipline at the Royal Military College would do me a lot of good - and I suppose it did."

southern England. From Plymouth, after a few days respite, the unit was moved by train to Shorncliffe on the Kent coast. It was here that reality began to set in.

The unceasing rain that had followed the unit across the Atlantic turned their makeshift camp into a sea of mud as canvas leaked like muslin and the ground became a slippery quagmire. Waiting to cross the English Channel it seemed a dismal prelude to an uncertain future. Already the high casualty lists were dulling the keen edge of warmongery so eagerly practised by a once innocent public when war began on August 4, 1914. The steady flow of the injured and the dying had turned into a torrent of wounded shipped back from the continent to hospitals in England. Signs that it was not a 'lovely war' were everywhere.

66 We Canadians will never forget the thrill of those first days of the war, and then the terrible waiting before most of us could get to the other side. Our great fear was that the fighting would all be over before we could give a hand in it. How little we knew then of the glory that was to be Canada's in the story of the Western Front, of the sacrifices that were to reach to nearly every fireside in the Dominion!
For many months my bit seemed to consist of training, more training, delays and more delays. But at last we got over. We crossed in an old-time cattle-boat. Oh, what a trip! Fifteen days to reach England! We had 700 horses on board, and 700 seasick horses are not the most congenial steamer company.99

Bishop saw this clearly and, waiting to be shipped to the Western Front, he felt a despondent malaise that the prospect of trench warfare in France did little to improve. Neither was there much indication that the war would soon be over, although at first it had been thought that Christmas 1914 would see peace once more. Now, in the early summer of 1915 the bitter struggle had been fought for almost a year and a stalemate had descended upon the millions massed for conflict as they waited in mile upon mile of trench lines that split the continent.

Like two giant battering rams the Central Powers comprising Germany and the Austro-Hungarian Empire and the Allied Powers of Britain, France and Russia, pushed and pressed upon each other for yards of territory here and there at the cost of thousands upon thousands of lives. Just hours after Germany declared war on France on August 1, 1914, more than 500 trains a day began moving troops to the French and Belgian borders until 1.5 million men stood ready to put Field Marshal Count Alfred von Schlieffen's war plan into action.

It was to have been a lightning strike west and south-west through Holland and Belgium and south from the coast by-passing the massive French fortifications. In six weeks France was to be overwhelmed, whereupon the efficient German railways, so carefully developed with this purpose in mind, would quickly shift German troops to the east for an attack on Russia before that country could fully mobilise. Masterminded by the Prussians, Europe's most efficient and feared fighting force since the Napoleonic Wars, their skills honed by the Franco-Prussian War of 1870, Germany's plan for its great enveloping conquest of continental Europe unfolded.

But critical elements in von Schlieffen's plan were changed. Instead of strengthening the right for the sweep around by the English Channel, the German Chief of Staff, von Moltke, added divisions to the left to prevent the French cutting up into Germany; and when Russia attacked in the east he lost his nerve and began shifting troops to that front. The Germans met their fate at Mons where the British turned and stood their ground, and again at the Marne where the first strategic counter-offensive took place, preventing the occupation of Paris. It quickly developed into a standing confrontation, each side digging in to the soil of France and Flanders.

It was just the beginning of a war that would last four more years and take the lives of almost 13 million men in the armed forces of the Central and Allied Powers, and a further 13 million civilians after that, victims of a virulent influenza caused by the apalling conditions. Sucked into the thin vacuum of death that sandwiched no-man's land between ranks of opposing trenches, men came from half way around the world to be fed into the giant threshing machine of destruction. It was to this unhappy mess that Billy Bishop would soon be delivered and he sensed the inevitability of that awful fate.

Depressed and soaked to the skin, Billy Bishop pondered on the consequences as he ploughed his way through mud up to his knees to inspect the horses on the line one day in July. He would soon leave the south coast of England for France. It had been raining for days and a seeping drizzle gave little respite as he squelched and plodded through the stinking bog of mud and excrement from the horses that he knew would be his to tend in the much worse conditions of the Western Front.

Unexpectedly, a Nieuport biplane flew in and landed on clear ground some short distance away from Bishop. In that moment he made up his mind to seek escape from the defecating horses and mud lined trenches by getting a transfer to the Royal Flying Corps. In Folkestone he fell in among a group of RFC officers where he learned about Lord Hugh Cecil at the War Office in London who, reputedly, could arrange transfers to the Flying Corps. Before he could do much about it, Bishop again went down with pneumonia and after a spell in hospital went to London to convalesce.

Booking into a room at the Royal Automobile Club, he could once again pursue his intended transfer to the Flying Corps. Bishop wanted to be a trainee pilot and presented himself for that role when he sought out Lord Cecil, who was not usually

"We were very proud to be in England. We felt we were really in the war-zone, and soon would be in the fighting. But it is a great mistake to think that when you sail from America you are going to burst right up to the front and go over the top at daybreak in the morning. The way to the war is long. There was more work and more training for us in England. At first we were sent to a very sandy camp on the coast, and from there to a very muddy camp somewhere else in the British Isles."

Right

As an observer, Bishop's job was to carry out reconnaissance from the front seat of the R.E.7 and, if necessary, fend off attack. He never got the chance to engage the enemy until he gained his wings and joined No. 60 Sqdn, RFC, as a pilot.

66 *The day for your trip over happens to be one of wondrous sunshine and the clearest possible visibility. At every aerodrome behind the long British war-line the aeroplanes are out of their hangars, and are being tested with such a babel of noisy explosions that in moving about with a companion you have fairly to shout to make yourself heard. With your pilot you climb into the waiting two-seater. It has been groomed for the day and fussed over with as much care as a mother might bestow upon her only offspring starting for Sunday school.* **99**

approached by Canadians on impromptu visits to the War Office. Nevertheless, Cecil was impressed, and informed Bishop that if he wanted to become a pilot he would have to wait at least six months. However, if he would settle for becoming an observer, he could transfer right away. Bishop was in a quandry: was he merely exchanging one boring job for another, or should he settle for being an observer and learn to become a pilot once he had settled in?

Back at Shorncliffe, Bishop's C.O. had no doubts: he should transfer to the RFC as an observer. Bishop acted promptly, and was sent to Netheravon on September 1, 1915. Located on Salisbury Plain about 11 miles north of the town of Salisbury in Wiltshire, Netheravon had long been associated with flying at a time when the activity was still relatively new. Less than three miles to the south, at a place called Larkhill, the War Office had set up a small shed in 1910 for the Hon. Charles Rolls, who was to teach officers to fly.

Less than seven years earlier Orville Wright had been the first man to fly a powered aeroplane in controlled flight and although aeroplanes were considered potentially useful for observation purposes, their prospective military role was confined to supporting ground operations. In April 1912 the Royal Flying Corps had been formed with a Military Wing and a Naval Wing. A Central Flying School would train pilots for both operational Wings. Now it was time to select aeroplanes for the RFC, and, two years to the month before Germany declared war on France and Belgium, the British Army held what it called a Military Aeroplane Competition on Salisbury Plain. Thirty-two different types entered the contest, although eight failed to arrive.

There were biplanes, monoplanes, pusher aeroplanes with the engine behind, and tractor powered aeroplanes with the engine in front. Aeroplanes came from France as well as England and

Below
An R.E.7 reconnaissance biplane equipped with the RAF 4a engine. Underpowered throughout its life, the aircraft gave Bishop his first taste of operational flying.

there was even an entrant from Austria-Hungary. One of those entered by The Aircraft Manufacturing Co. Ltd., set up by George Holt for the manufacture of aeroplanes built by the brothers Henry and Maurice Farman, would be a precursor to the Maurice Farman that took Billy Bishop on his first aerial excursion at Netheravon three years later. The English brothers Henry and Maurice Farman took up French citizenship and developed a family of biplanes that were purchased in large numbers for the RFC.

The Series 7 entered in the military trials of 1912 was not well placed by the judges, yet would more than prove its worth. In 1913 the Series 11 appeared devoid of a forward elevator carried on booms ahead of the wings and nacelle carrying the pilot. To some, the protruding booms looked for all the world like the horns of Highland cattle. Without booms for elevators, the Series 7 had only the much shorter, forward projecting skids. It was quickly dubbed Shorthorn while its progenitor was known as the Longhorn! It was on the Shorthorn that Bishop first came to flying and the exhilarating experience of surging through the air, albeit at no more than 70 mph, the top speed of the biplane.

66 It was to this camp that the aeroplane came that stormy day in July. A week later my plans were in motion. I met a friend in the Royal Flying Corps and confided in him my ambition to fly. He assured me it would be easy to arrange a transfer, and instructed me as to what I should do. If I wanted to get to the front quickly I would have to go as an observer, meaning that when I flew over the German lines I would be the 'passenger' in a two-seated plane and would do just what my title indicated - observe.
If one has a stomach for flying, it doesn't take long to become a fairly competent observer. There are observer schools where they teach you just what to observe and what not to observe. This is not a joke. If an observer lets his gaze wander to too many non-essentials he cannot do the real observing that is expected of him.99

Powered by a 80 hp Renault rotary engine, the Shorthorn carried its crew in tandem, the observer in front and the pilot behind suspended mid-way between the wings in a nacelle looking like a bathtub. The observer had a splendid view forward, down and all around the sky, and attempts to fit a Lewis machine gun had been made by the Royal Aircraft Factory the previous year.

The first Shorthorns had served with No. 6 Sqdn, RFC, before war broke out but none were sent to France when the first four squadrons left on August 14. Some did go soon after, however, and a handful were still struggling on in September 1915, when Bishop was at Netheravon. But the type was clearly useless against the mounting opposition, especially from the single-seat Fokker monoplanes that had begun to appear over the Western Front. It became increasingly useful as a trainer and as a vehicle for initiating recruits as observers. It certainly impressed Bishop:

66 I loved those first few flights in an old training bus. I don't think she made more than fifty miles per hour; and as for climbing, she struggled and shook and gasped like a freight train going up a mountain side. But it was thrilling enough for me in those days, despite the fact that I soon began to envy the pilot who had all the fun of running the machine and could make it do a few lame and decrepit stunts. 99

Bishop's first assignment as an observer was with No. 21 Sqdn, RFC, also based at Netheravon, which was formed on July 23, 1915, from No. 8 Reserve Aeroplane Squadron. The reserve squadrons were training units from which were formed operational squadrons, each formally designated with a specific number by which it would be identified in the field. Consequently, No. 8 RNAS became No. 21 Sqdn, RFC, and would be known as such until finally disbanded in 1976. The squadron also received its first aircraft during late July, the R.E.7, with which the unit would work up for offensive duty in France.

Every day, pilots and observers took to the air over Salisbury Plain to practise the art of flying reconnaissance missions and the science of aerial photography and wireless transmissions in morse code. The R.E.7 derived its designation from the codes of aircraft types applied to products of the Royal Aircraft Factory. It stood for Reconnaissance Experimental and was the seventh type designated as such. Some types evolved from series of aircraft inspired by other manufacturers in other countries. For instance, the B.E. series were designated from the Bleriot Experimental family, the F.E. from the Farman Experimental, the S.E. from the Santos Experimental, and so on although they were all designed at Farnborough.

66 Christmas Day we cooked our own turkey and the rest of the meal. Then, in a burst of Yuletide hospitality, we telephoned to a local hotel and told the manager to send anybody he wanted to out to the aerodrome for dinner. Alas for our ten-pound turkey! The guests from the hotel kept coming until there were actually twenty of them. However, in some miraculous way, we managed to feed the hungry score. Having partaken of our food, they did not tarry long. Night shut in early and once more we took up our wintry vigil.99

The R.E.1 first appeared in July 1913 and was a two-seat tractor biplane, as was the R.E.7 that Bishop trained on. It was very different to the Shorthorn and had the appearance of a modern and very capable aeroplane. With covered-in fuselage, an in-line engine in front of the observer's seat and the pilot behind, it had two forward skids projecting from two oleo legs which telescoped on the ground to support the aircraft's weight but extended, dangling like the legs of a crane fly, when the R.E.7 became airborne. The field of view for the observer and, for that matter the pilot too, was not as good as it had been on the Shorthorn, but the R.E.7 was powered by a 120 hp Beardmore engine and could supposedly carry a modest bomb load as well as defensive armament.

The first year of war brought the first formal modifications in design to aircraft intended to operate on observation and reconnaissance duty. Fighters were appearing over the Western Front with the specific purpose of attacking other aeroplanes and the observer had need of a gun with which to fend off assailants. But the R.E.7 was dangerously underpowered, as demonstrated during its first action over the Western Front in early October 1915. Unable to load it with the bombs it was designed to carry, the RFC pressed it into service as an escort fighter.

Overleaf
A rare photograph of an R.E.5 specially modified at Farnborough, England, for experiments with a 336lb bomb. The plane appears to have the wings of an R.E.4 and the undercarriage and fin of an R.E.7!

Loaded only with an observer and his armament it had passable credibility but with a top speed of just over 70 mph at 5,000 feet, an altitude which it took more than 30 minutes to reach, the aircraft was in fact a sitting duck. The few that had been tried out with No. 12 Sqdn were to be withdrawn as No. 21 went to France fully equipped with aircraft of this type. As the then Brig.-Gen. Hugh M. Trenchard, in charge of RFC Headquarters, wrote: "I do not propose to keep up the R.E.7 machines in No. 12 Sqdn after the first squadron of R.E.7s has arrived."

So it was that No. 21 left for France by sea on January 17, 1916, as a new squadron which would pioneer the operational debut of a dubious tool for reconnaissance and bombing. And Billy Bishop was finally going to war, seven months after arriving in England from Canada. The men and materiel went by sea, as did the crated aeroplanes, and the two rendezvoused at Boisdinghem about six miles west of St. Omer to formally set up the squadron from January 23. It was dismal weather. Sleet and snow made flying difficult, especially with underpowered machines which were all but useless for the job at hand.

66 After a few months I was graduated as an observer and was awarded my first insignia of the Flying Corps - an O, with one outstretched wing attached to it, to be worn on the left breast of the tunic. I was rather proud of that one wing, but more determined than ever to win the double wings of a fully fledged pilot, and some day have a machine of my own.99

Attempting to justify its design, the Royal Aircraft Factory proudly announced that improvements in performance could be achieved with the R.E.7 by removing the silencer for the Beardmore engine and fitting six separate exhaust stubs. Trenchard was not impressed and sent a rejoinder to the effect that "the R.E.7 is underpowered to such an extent that the effect of 5 per cent extra horse power will be negligible," and that he did not intend hampering field operations by ordering such a pointless and time consuming modification.

Bishop and his fellow squadron personnel were under the command of Maj. Richey, as part of the newly formed GHQ Wing along with No. 12 Sqdn at St. Omer, under the control of the General Officer Commanding, Royal Flying Corps. The two squadrons were to carry out special strategic and patrol work for headquarters. Bishop was not enamoured with the R.E.7:

66 It was a machine designed to mount four guns, cameras and all manner of other equipment including a 500 pound bomb (actually a 336 lb bomb - ed.) *lashed to the fuselage. The idea was to fly over the target, take a quick look over the side of the cockpit, pull the wire cable - and away the bomb would go. All that was wrong was that this machine stoutly refused to leave the ground when all this gear, plus the pilot and observer, were packed into it.*

66 The first time we tried to take up our R.E.7, Roger Neville gunned across Boisdinghem at least a dozen times into the wind, but the wheels never left the ground. Consultation followed. They decided that we should try and get airborne without the bomb. The wheels bounced a few times, but we still weren't in the air at the point on the runway where we would have to throttle down and turn around to avoid running off the field. More consultation.

" They decided to move us to a larger field at St. Omer, ten miles away, in the hope that with a longer run the R.E.7 might consent to struggle into the air. Finally we succeeded, but only after removing two of the four machine guns as well. "

During February the squadron carried out patrols from St. Omer to the North Sea coast. The fear of attack from Fokker monoplanes was endemic, and the squadron was also used for escort duty. A typical sortie on February 7 involved a single B.E.2c reconnaissance machine, to which four R.E.7s from No. 21 Sqdn were assigned, together with three B.E.2cs, two F.E.s and a Bristol Scout from No. 12 Sqdn, and two F.E.s from the Second Wing. In all, twelve aeroplanes were escort to one two-seat machine which failed anyway to make the appropriate reconnaissance.

Such was the fear of attack from Fokker monoplanes, equipped with synchronised machine guns firing forward through the propeller arc, thus enabling the pilot to point the aircraft at the target and pull the trigger to effect a kill. No more manoeuvering for a slant-angle deflection shot from a second crew member exposed in an open cockpit. The day of the single-seat fighter - the machine that Bishop would use with great skill and talent - had arrived.

" In a very short time I was in France and ready for my first trip over the enemy lines. As I look back upon it now my life as an observer seems very tame. The work of the reconnaissance and artillery machines, as well as the photography and bombing planes, is very important. It goes on day and night, in good weather and bad, but all the times I was observing I wanted to be fighting. Whenever I saw one of the small, swift, single-seater machines, which were just coming into vogue then for fighting purposes, my resolve to become a fighting pilot would grow stronger and stronger."

The following month activity continued but the underpowered aircraft were unable to carry out their duties properly. On March 8, Trenchard reported that he was, "of the opinion that the R.E.7 with 120 hp Beardmore engine is useless in the field. The lifting power of the machine rapidly decreases, and although the engines appear to be running now better than they ever did and every care has been given to looking at the propellers, the fact remains that not half of the machines can get off the ground if it is at all sticky with full loads, nor can they climb to 8,000 ft. Therefore, I shall be glad to have these machines replaced at an early date."

What constituted major problems and irritation to Bishop and his fellow aviators and frustration for Trenchard was merely one more indication of unsatisfactory equipment to the architects of air power and strategy in England. They had many priorities, and the pace of the development of roles and applications for military aircraft could not be matched by the design and engineering necessary to produce the new aircraft required. In the majority of cases a compromise was the only solution. In this instance Billy Bishop got to fly R.E.7s with better engines, but replacements for that aircraft would have to wait until better designs came along.

On April 2, 1916, the squadron moved to St-Andre-aux-Bois. The new engines were 140 hp R.A.F.4a types which gave a marginal improvement in performance, but serious lubrication problems kept the squadron mostly grounded during the month. On May 7, the C.O., Maj. R. Campbell-Heathcote, could report that five out of his seven aircraft were unserviceable. It was an unhappy time for the squadron and a distinctly unlucky period for Bishop. Frequently called upon to ride shot-gun for B.E.2 reconnaissance machines, his role had been transformed from one of aerial observer to air gunner by the underpowered aircraft and their vulnerability to the Fokker monoplanes' synchronised machine guns.

It is no child's play to circle above a German battery observing for half an hour or more, with the machine tossing about in air, tortured by exploding shells and black shrapnel puffballs coming nearer and nearer to you like the ever-extending finger-tips of some giant hand of death. But it is just a part of the never-ceasing war. In the air service this work is never done. Everywhere along the line the big guns wait daily for the wireless touch of aeroplanes to set them booming at targets carefully selected from a previous day of observation. Big shells cannot be wasted. The human effort involved in creating them and placing them beside the well-screened guns at the front is far too great for that.

No. 21 Sqdn was one of the first RFC squadrons equipped with synchronising gear when, along with Nos. 70 and 19 Squadrons, they became the first British units to operate guns firing through the propeller arc. That was in August, two months after the Somme offensive began and three months after Bishop left for England on leave. No. 21 suffered heavily in their R.E.7s, which they finally exchanged in July for single-seat B.E.12 biplanes. On June 19 the squadron had been moved south to the Somme valley, and had Bishop remained with the unit he would probably have been killed as a sitting duck in an outmoded aeroplane that should have been withdrawn months earlier.

During the closing weeks of his first operational tour Bishop participated in the run-up to the great Somme offensive commanded by General Sir Henry Rawlinson. The artillery barrage orchestrated as a prelude would unleash 2 million shells from 1,400 heavy guns in seven days; almost 200 shells a minute non-stop night and day for a week. What Bishop would be mercifully spared were the endless flights back and forth across the lines to railway stations held by the Germans, enemy ammunition dumps and stores containing shells; places conveniently covered with tarpaulins bearing a large red cross!

The slow, underpowered, over-loaded biplanes struggled against the concussion of air-bursts from artillery shells, furious attacks from German fighters, and the ever present threat that their engines would simply seize up due to their poor and inefficient lubrication system. What No. 21 Sqdn endured during late June and July helped sustain first the intense barrage and then the human assault that on the first day alone caused almost 60,000 British casualties; more in fact than Britain had ever suffered before, or would suffer in any one day during two world wars.

As many British soldiers were killed in those few hours on the Somme as there were civilian dead throughout the British Isles in more than 2,000 days of World War II. In all, British, French and German casualties during the Somme offensive totalled almost 1,300,000 men, and at the end a report from the Imperial General Staff in London concluded that: "The Powers...are beginning to get a little uneasy...The casualties are beginning to mount up and (we are) wondering whether we are likely to get a proper return for them...with no very great gains."

The year had been earmarked by the Allies as the year for supreme effort. It became the year of greatest sacrifice in the history of warfare. Bishop was well out of it, but if unscathed in battle he seemed peculiarly prone to illness and accident. During April Bishop was severely shaken when a truck he was travelling in collided with another truck; then he was hit by part of an aircraft and concussed for 48 hours. A week after recovering from that he went down with a mouth infection which put him back in hospital, only to suffer a knee injury during a heavy landing soon after discharge.

In May he was sent back to England on sick leave, where he was supposed to rest up and mend. Spirits were high. He was escaping the endless cycle of death and destruction for a while and it was time for merry-making. Not that squadron life had been devoid of fun. Putting together a revue which was performed by squadron officers in front of the visiting Brig.-Gen. Brooke-Popham, things got out of hand when the renditions became a little too explicit and it was banned as being immoral! On the steamer taking him back home, anticipation of leave and all that implied was too much to withstand without a drink, and Bishop finally arrived at Folkestone in no fit state to make it down the gangplank.

Claiming he was pushed, he fell and added further injury to his partially healed knee. Disinclined to rest and recuperate, Bishop set about a swashbuckling indulgence of London and its vibrant night life, only reporting to the RFC hospital in Bryanston Square near Marble Arch two days before his scheduled return

Every day there are hundreds of photographs to be taken, so that the British map-makers can trace each detail of the German trench positions and can check any changes in the enemy zone. Information is to be gained at all times by all manner of reconnaissances - some of them carrying you fifty to sixty miles in the enemy country. Then, there is the fighting patrol work which goes on all hours. The patrol is not on our side of the line. It is far over the German lines to keep the enemy machines from coming too close even to their own front trenches. Of course they do slip over occasionally, but more than often have to pay for their temerity.

Every shell must be watched. It is a startling thing, but true. When we possess the high ground and the ridges, it is not always necessary for the aeroplanes or the balloons to do the observing; the artillery observing officers can go forward on the ground and from a convenient tree-top, a bit of trench, or a sheltering shell-hole see exactly what his guns are doing.

Altogether I spent four months in France as an observer. How I longed during all that time for a fight in the air! But no real chances came, and, finally, I quitted my seat as a passenger without having fired a single combat shot from the the tidy little machine gun that was always near me and seemed to yearn as much as I did to have a go at the enemy.

to France. The doctors examining his knee noted the severity of the injury but they also detected a heart murmur and immediately confined him to bed.

For some weeks Bishop remained in the care and custody of the medical staff. It was customary for patients in the hospital to receive visitors who provided a social service of friendship and support for RFC personnel recovering sometimes from the worst of injuries. One such person was the 69 year old Lady St. Helier, who had a fashionable home in Portland Place. On seeing his name on the patient roster, and thinking Billy to be related to a Will Bishop she had met before, she approached him and confirmed that Will and Billy were indeed members of the same family.

When sufficiently well to leave the RFC Hospital, Bishop took up Lady St. Helier's offer of a room in her home where he could rest and recuperate. She may even have pulled strings to get him evacuated back to Canada on indefinite leave where, after almost a year away from home, he was glad to be back among his family and friends. For Billy Bishop the war could have been over. It would not have been difficult to play upon his heart condition or his knee injury for a sustained spell of convalescence. But this was not the future Billy Bishop saw for himself. He had sat too long in the front seat of an R.E.7 not to dream of the chance of handling the controls and flying the aeroplane himself. Resolved to become a pilot, he returned to England in September 1916.

CHAPTER THREE *Wings of Victory*

Billy Bishop's hopes of becoming a pilot were rudely dashed when he arrived in London for a succession of interviews where he was repeatedly rejected as medically unfit. Lodging again with Lady St. Helier, he decided to recruit her to his cause. Her influence, whatever it was, paid off and Bishop was given the most cursory examination from which he was passed as fit for training. Then it was off to Oxford, and Brasenose College, for his first courses of instruction. While there in October 1916 amid a class full of students who had been neither in the air nor on operational duty, he shone. Then it was back to Salisbury Plain and Upavon on November 1, 1916, for his first flying lessons.

❝ This consisted, first of all, in going up in another old machine - a steady type called the Maurice Farman, and fitted with a dual set of controls, so that the instructor could manage one while I tried to manage the other. Never will I forget those days of dual control. I tried very hard, but it seemed to me that I just couldn't get the proper feel of the machine. First the instructor would tell me I was ham-handed - that I gripped the controls too tightly with every muscle tense.

❝ After that I would what you might call get timid-handed, and not hold the controls tightly enough. My instructor and I suffered tortures. So when suddenly one day he told me I could go up alone, I had my doubts as to whether it was confidence or desperation that dictated his decision. I didn't worry long as to which it was; I was willing to take the chance. ❞

For a World War I aviator, this was the most dangerous period of his predictably short life. More casualties were incurred in training than on operations. Flying training was not the science it would quickly become after the war. Instructors were mostly old pilots resting from the battle in France and Flanders, or young men with little more experience than the newly passed pilot about to join his first squadron. Few instructors encouraged their pupils to get 'hands-on' experience because the machines they used for tuition were old, in poor condition or un-airworthy wrecks posing a danger to life and limb. The inexperienced could wreak havoc in such machines!

Somehow, Bishop passed the first crucial solo test and although he crash-landed the Maurice Farman, went on to make good progress. He joined a home defence squadron at Northolt just outside London for advanced training prior to getting his wings. He only just managed to achieve this before his C.O., Maj. B. F. Moore, ensured that he was rapidly posted; this time to No. 37 (Home Defence) Sqdn, RFC, operating from Sutton's Farm on the banks of the Thames east of London.

Bishop was to spend many hours flying at night over southern England, putting this time to good use in practising and improving his flying. Already, just since December 1914, there had been 42 raids by airships and 25 attacks by aeroplanes. In total, 160 airships and 39 aeroplanes had dropped 164.5 tons of

❝ Then followed my first solo! This is, I think, the greatest day in a flying man's life. Certainly I did not stop talking about it for the next three weeks at least, I felt a great and tender pity for all the millions of people in the world who never have a chance to do a solo!

An ambulance stood in the aerodrome, and it seemed to me, as it has to many another student-pilot, that all the other business of flying had suddenly ceased so that everybody could look at me. I noticed with a shiver that the ambulance had its engine running. Were the doctors at the hospital expectantly fondling their knives? Everybody looked cold-blooded and heartless. But I had to do it: so into the machine I crawled, trying to look cheerful, but feeling awfully lonesome. How I got off the ground I do not know, but once in the air it was not nearly so bad - not much worse than the first time you started down-hill on an old-fashioned bicycle.❞

❝ For a time I felt very much pleased with myself circling above the aerodrome, but suddenly an awful thought came to me. Somehow or other I had to get that machine down to the earth again. How blissful it would be if I could just keep on flying! At last, however, I screwed up all my courage, reached for the throttle, pushed it back, and the engine almost stopped. I knew the next thing to do was to put her nose down. So down it went at a steep angle. I felt it was too steep, so I pulled her nose up a bit, then put it down again, and in a series of steps I had been told carefully to carry out, descended toward the ground.❞

bombs, killed 520 people and caused damage amounting to £1.5 million. Responding to hysterical reaction from Londoners who earlier in the war had rioted and marched on the War Office demanding protection, aircraft badly needed on the Western Front were held back for the air defence of Britain.

Since most attacks were made by night it was at night the pilots had to fly, although Bishop's flights were on routine practice or test; he was never sent up against an airship or an aeroplane in the two months he served at Sutton's Farm. Night flying was very different, as Bishop recalled when describing one such mission during his final stages of flying training at Northolt:

66One other machine was up at the same time, doing its test, and somehow, although the space in the air is very wide, I had a great fear that we might collide, so I gazed anxiously out into the darkness trying to see the little navigation lights we carried on our wings. It is hard to look into jet blackness, and the strain hurt my eyes, but I was afraid not to look for all I was worth. I continued to fly as far as possible in a dead straight line. 99

He was fascinated by the thrill of flying a machine over which he had total control, that was in effect a night fighter equipped to shoot down German aircraft and airships. *66I spent hours practising in the air both by day and by night. Several times we had flight manoeuvres at night, and that was ticklish work. We would go up to patrol a certain area with lights showing on all the aerodromes in that section of the country, so that you could steer by them.*

66I don't know of many greater tests of a pilot's skill than this flying in the dark, with a lot of machines about you in the air, their little navigation lights looking for all the world like so many moving stars. The cold of the higher altitudes at night is agonisingly intense. After half an hour or so in the frigid zone you get sort of numb and then for a long while the cold doesn't seem to affect you any more. The real nasty part is when you have landed and begin to thaw out. It is really worse than the original freezing. 99

For all the hardship of night patrols in the middle of winter, Bishop was seduced by the sights only night pilots experienced. *66In spite of the discomforts and the dangers of night flying you could not fail to admire the great beauty of the scene below you when the lights were on and sparkling. These lights would mean nothing to a stranger, but to us in the air they were friendly beacons of safety and gave us a feeling of absolute security.*

66I held the controls very carefully and kept my eyes glued to the instruments that gleamed brightly under little electric bulbs inside the machine. I could not see a thing around me; only the stars overhead. Underneath there was a great black void. After flying straight forwards for several minutes I summoned up courage enough to make a turn. I carefully and gradually rounded the corner, and away off to one side I could see the flares on the ground. I completed a big circuit and shut off the engine preparatory to landing. Suddenly, in the midst of my descent, I realised I had misjudged it very badly, so quickly put the engine on again and proceeded to fly around a second time. Then I came down, and, to my intense surprise, made quite a good landing. This was only the beginning. I had to repeat the trick several times.99

66On the final test I had to attain a given height. I left the ground as before, and just as I did so could see the reflection of the flares on the tin roofs of our huts. It made a great impression upon me, as I climbed away into the darkness. Then my thoughts went to my engine and I realised it was as important as my own heart. I listened to its steady beat with an anxious ear. Once or twice there was a slight kick or hitch in its smooth rhythm. No matter how many cylinders you have whirring in front of you, the instant one misses your heart hears it even before your ears do. Several times my heart seemed to stop. The tension became very great as I toiled and struggled up through the night. The lack of anything upon which I could put my eyes outside the machine gave me a very queer feeling.99

Far left
Gaining his wings and qualifying as a pilot gave Bishop the freedom he wanted to pursue his lone war against the enemy.

"My luck as a Zeppelin hunter was very poor. I used to dream occasionally about stalking the great monsters in the high thin air, pouring a drum of blazing bullets into them and gloating as they flared into flame. But no real Zeppelins ever came my way. The cold nights that we stood by on duty waiting for them were very long, but not without their compensations. There would be two of us at a given station. We would play cards, strum on some sort of instrument read for an hour or so, play cards again, and all the while hoping for an alarm that would send us aloft in pursuit of a marauding gasbag from over the sea."

"On such nights the skies would seem full to overflowing with myriad stars. We finally became so accustomed to flying in the dark that nothing troubled us except ground mists or light fogs that would occasionally slip in from the sea, obliterate the lights, and make a landing a difficult and perilous task."

But even this was not sufficient to hold Bishop's interest for long. He hated inactivity and soon became bored with the enforced wait for German aircraft and airships that never seemed to come. In reality, there was a lull in German air raids, although they did begin to pick up again during February. By that time Bishop had made several attempts to get transferred to the Western Front where he would be sure of more action:

"Toward the end of February word came through from the War Office one night that I was to go to France. I had become convinced that the winter would not offer much opportunity at Zeppelin hunting, and had applied several times for duty at the fighting front. Before I went, however, there was another course at a special school, where I learned to fly the smallest of our single-seater machines.

"Now, I felt, I had reached the height of my ambition at last; actually to fly one of these tiny, wasp-like fighting machines seemed to me the most wonderful thing in the world. A few days later, when I reported for my orders to cross the Channel it was with a gay heart, and a determination to reflect as much honour as I could upon the double wings on my left breast."

Billy Bishop was posted to No. 60 Sqdn, RFC, then based at Filescamp Farm, which was the eastern part of le Hameau aerodrome, located about twelve miles west of Arras. No. 60 Sqdn had been formed during March 1916 at Gosport from the nucleus of No. 1 Reserve Squadron (the original designation RAS being abbreviated to RS in January 1916) and embarked for St. Omer at the end of May. Equipped with Morane Saulnier monoplanes it made several moves before settling at Savy in September.

"The first day of my stay with the squadron there was no flying, and so I wandered about the field hangars looking at the machines. They were all of a type I had never seen before at close range - Nieuport Scouts, very small and, of course, with but a single seat. Being a French model, the Nieuport Scout is a beautiful creature. The distinctly British machines - and some of our newer ones are indeed marvels of the air - are built strictly for business, with no particular attention paid to the beauty of the lines. The French, however, never overlook such things."

Prior to that, No. 60 had been retired to rest up at St. Andre-aux-Bois just three miles from Hesdin. Flying Morane parasol monoplanes, where the single wing was held above the slim fuselage on struts giving it the appearance of a parasol, and Morane types N, I and V, the unit had suffered heavy casualties. Maj.-Gen. Trenchard wrote Sir Douglas Haig upon resting No. 60 that "This squadron... has lost a Squadron Commander, two of its Flight Commanders and one pilot killed or missing and yesterday it lost two more machines with two pilots and observers to anti-aircraft fire."

When operations resumed Albert Ball joined the squadron, a free-wheeling young pilot, then only 19 years old, who was quickly recognised as an individual of outstanding ability. He was given a roving commission and allowed to come and go as he pleased, usually on missions to shoot down German aircraft with great efficiency. No. 60 fought successfully through hard days as the second and third battles of the Somme dragged on into autumn 1916, having received in August the nimble and spirited little Nieuport 16 and 17 sesquiplanes.

Maintaining the precedent set by the Moranes, No. 60 continued to operate French aircraft and were the first RFC squadron to be fully equipped with Nieuports. The squadron moved to Filescamp Farm on January 16, 1917, with snow on the ground and a hard frost most nights. Here Billy Bishop joined the unit on March 9. He was accompanied by Denis Townesend who had been with Bishop at the Royal Military College in Ontario. Their newly appointed C.O. was Maj. A. J. L. Scott who had been a successful barrister in London before the war.

Lamed in a hunting accident, Scott had difficulty in walking and had to taxi his aircraft unusually close to his squadron office to be lifted bodily from his aircraft. He was a generous man, a father-figure warmly respected by the young pilots. He nurtured their loyalty and support by giving in return his own commitment to the squadron and its record. The young pilots knew they could rely on his support both personally and in his projection of the squadron's best image. Maj. Scott keenly encouraged his men to engage and shoot down the enemy, thus improving their own record as well as that of the squadron.

Bishop joined No. 60 at an interesting time in the air war. The Albatros biplanes, their design inspired by the sesquiplane configuration of the tiny Nieuport, were becoming a major force in the German Army Air Service and the Allies had few aircraft that could match them in combat. Bishop went out on his first patrol on March 17, 1917, in Nieuport Type 17 serial number A274. The aircraft left the ground at 10:10 am and were back just two hours later. The pilots had seen hostile aircraft but had been unable to engage them.

Six days later Bishop was up again with a patrol which had to return due to poor weather, and a day later two afternoon patrols were made followed by a short fifteen minute flight on the

66 We newcomers at the squadron - the other pilot and myself - had to stand by the next day and watch the patrols leaving to do their work over the lines. It was thrilling even to us, accustomed as we were to ordinary flying, to see the trim little fighters take the air, one after the other, circle above the aerodrome, and then, dropping into a fixed formation, set their courses to the east. That night we listened with eager ears to the discussion of a fight in which a whole patrol had been engaged. We stay-at-homes had spent the day practise-flying in the new machines. There were three days more of this for me, and then, having passed some standard tests to show my familiarity with the Nieuport type, I was told the next morning I was to cross the lines for the first time as the master of my own machine.99 morning of the 25th. Then, at 4:15 pm that afternoon, in Nieuport 17 A6693, Bishop took off with his patrol and climbed through low clouds and mist toward St. Leger where they found three Albatros scouts. The German biplanes dived to attack them and it was soon a free-for-all as each aeroplane bucked and weaved for position.

Bishop quickly attached himself to one and followed it down through cloud where he fired brief bursts from his wing-mounted Lewis gun. The Albatros kept on diving and struck the ground out of control. Then, climbing back up again, Bishop was horrified when, full of lubricating oil, his engine suddenly stopped dead in the air:

Below

The Nieuport sesquiplane was to achieve prominent success for the French manufacturer and inspire the Germans to produce copies, most used of which were the Albatros D.III and D.V./Va series.

"I tried every trick I knew to coax a fresh start, but it was no use. I had no choice. I had to land in the country directly beneath me, be it hostile or friendly. I turned in what seemed to me by instinct to be the way toward our lines, and glided as far as I could without any help from the engine. I saw beneath me a destroyed village, and my heart sank. I must be behind the German lines. Was my real flying career, just begun, to be ended so soon?...Mechanically, without realising just what I was doing, but all the time following that first great instinct of self-preservation, I remember carefully picking out a clear path in the rough terrain beneath me, and making a last turn, I glided into it and landed."

Right
Billy Bishop quickly found in aerial combat a self confessed satisfaction that transformed the job into a game which he relished and would recall with affection throughout his life.

66 It is great fun to fly very low along the German trenches and give them a burst of machine-gun bullets as a greeting in the morning, or a good-night salute in the evening. They don't like it a bit. But we love it; we love to see the Kaiser's proud Prussians running for cover like so many rats.
Whatever your mission, whether it is to direct artillery fire, to photograph, to bomb an ammunition-dump or supply-train, or just to look old Fritz over and see in a general way what he is up to, your first journey into Hunland is a memorable event in your life.99

Not knowing whether he had landed in German territory or not, Bishop leapt from his aircraft and ran for a ditch until friendly troops came by and he could emerge. He had landed just a few hundred feet from the front line. Two days later the Nieuport was retrieved by lorry and a number of mechanics that came to dismantle it, after Bishop had worked on the engine in soaking rain to free the clogged cylinders. When Billy Bishop filed his combat report it was approved as a credited victory, although the intelligence officer had first credited the enemy aircraft to a Lt. Bower:

Combats in the Air

Squadron: No. 60	*Date: 25-3-1917*
Type and No. of aeroplane: Nieuport Sct A306	*Time: 5 p.m.*
Armament: One Lewis Gun	*Duty: D.P.*
Pilot: Lieut. W. A. Bishop	*Height: 9,000 ft*
Observer: None	
Locality: Between St. Leger and Arras	

While on D.P. 3 Albatros Scouts approached us. One, separating from the rest, lost height and attempted to come up behind our second to the rear machine. I dived and fired about 12 to 15 rounds.

Tracers went all around his machine. He dived steeply for about 600 ft and flattened out. I followed him and opened fire from 40 to 50 yards range. A group of tracers went into the fuselage and centre section, one being seen to enter immediately behind the pilot's seat and one seemed to hit the pilot himself. The machine then fell out of control in a spinning nose dive. I dived after him, firing. I reached 1,500 or 2,000 ft. My engine had oiled up and I glided just over the lines at Sheet 51B T62D. The Albatros Scout when last seen by me was going vertically downwards at a height of 500 to 600 ft, evidently out of control, and appeared to crash at T5 or T11.

(Sgd) W. A. Bishop Lieut.

The day after Bishop returned to his squadron he led a patrol for the first time but had no luck. Two days later, on March 30, he was involved in a very unpleasant scrap when leading a flight of six aircraft that went to attack a lone German plane acting as decoy for ten Albatros scouts from Jagdstaffel 2. In the melee that followed, Lt. Garnett was shot down and 2nd/Lt. Bower received terrible injuries when an explosive bullet hit him, tore a hole in his stomach and put his aircraft into a spin. Holding his intestines in with one hand, he managed to fly away from the anti-aircraft fire and land. Bower climbed out of his aircraft, walked 100 feet and collapsed. He died in hospital the following day.

With one victory already confirmed, Billy Bishop wanted even more not only to avenge the death he now saw more directly than while flying reconnaissance machines, but also to increase his personal standing within the squadron. This was openly encouraged by Maj. Scott, who more than most C.O.s in the RFC would spur his men to personal achievement and merit where convention required modesty and team effort. The day 2nd/Lt. Bower succumbed to his injuries, Bishop got his second German:

“If it is artillery work you are on, you have learned to send down signals to your battery by means of a wireless buzzer, and you are equipped with intricate zone maps that enable you to pick out all manner of fixed objects in the enemy's domain. You can locate his dug-outs, his dumps, his lines of communication, his battery positions, his shelters behind the trees, and, in a general way, keep tab on his 'ways that are dark, and tricks that are vain.”

Combats in the Air

Squadron: No. 60
Type and No. of Aeroplane: Nieuport Scout A6769
Armament: One Lewis gun
Pilot: Lieut. W. A. Bishop
Observer: None
Locality: 10 mls N.E. of Arras
Remarks on Hostile Machine: 6 Albatros Scouts - 1 attacked

Date: 31-3-17
Time: 7:30 a.m.
Duty: Escort
Height: 10,000 ft

While on escort duty I went to the assistance of another Nieuport which was being attacked by an Albatros scout. I opened fire twice, the last time at 50 yards range. My tracers were seen to hit his machine in the centre section. The Albatros seemed to fall out of control, as he was in a spinning nose dive with his engine on. H.A. crashed at 7:30 am at Sheet 51B B29-30

(Sgd) W. W. Bishop Lieut.

I was behind Lieut. Bishop and saw the Albatros Scout go down in a spinning nose dive, seemingly out of control.

(Sgd) B. A. Leckie 2/Lt.

Maj. Scott added that the victory was also confirmed by the anti-aircraft batteries and consequently Bishop got his second kill. The first week of April brought new and expanded demands on the Royal Flying Corps as the Battle of Arras began. The Germans had pulled back to specially prepared defences awaiting the Allied assault and the air activity hotted up, beginning on the 4th, prior to the ground assault which was planned for the 9th; delayed by Nivelle, it finally began on the 15th.

On the other side of the lines, Manfred von Richthofen would lead the carnage meted out to the old, obsolete aircraft that formed the majority of British squadrons on the Western Front. In that month of 'Bloody April' he would shoot down 21 aircraft and extend his score to 52 confirmed victories (see Manfred von Richthofen, Famous Flyers No. 1). During March the RFC had lost 120 aircraft but in the first five days of the new offensive they lost 131 planes, of which 56 fell in accidents and were written off.

A variety of new Allied aircraft were coming into operational use, and although technically superior to some of the German scouts, they were not well known by the pilots assigned to fly them and were therefore not used optimally. One classic case was the Bristol F.2A two-seater. This was used much as two-seaters had been used all along: as a platform from which a rear gunner could defend the aircraft from marauding scouts, instead of as a truly omni-directional fighter where the pilot manoeuvred onto the enemy's tail, leaving the gunner to shoot at other aircraft as the opportunity arose.

But none of these concerns affected Billy Bishop. He had a nimble single-seater which, although beginning to look dated and perform less effectively than the latest German aircraft, was still a powerful little weapon in the hands of a dedicated fighter pilot. For several days in early April Billy Bishop tried to

improve his score. He was out every day, twice on April 2 when he lost his way and landed at Bruay, occupied by No. 16 Sqdn, almost ten miles north of Filescamp. Then, on April 6, he scored again:

Above
There is no record that Bishop ever fought Germany's top fighter ace Manfred von Richthofen (third from right) but he is known to have come up against pilots from von Richthofen's Jagdgeschwader Nr. 1. Note the parachute harness on the pilot at extreme right.

Combats in the Air

Squadron: No. 60
Type and No. of Aeroplane: Nieuport Scout A6769
Armament: One Lewis gun
Pilot: Lieut. W. A. Bishop
Observer: None
Locality: Sheet 51B 027/33; 28/34
Remarks on Hostile Machine: 1 Albatros Scout

Date: 6-4-17
Time: 9:35 a.m.
Duty: H.A.
Height: 15,000 ft

I engaged an Albatros Scout at 15,000 ft, diving at him from above and behind. I fired a burst of 15 to 20 rounds at 150 yards range, when the gun stopped. I dived again and opened fire at 10 yards range. He dived steeply and flattened out 1,000 ft lower. I opened fire again at 50 to 70 yards range. He dived steeply, but seemed to have his machine under control. I followed him down to 11,000 ft and he was still diving when I left him.

(Sgd) **W. A. Bishop Lieut.**

❝ *The scarlet machines of Baron von Richthofen's crack squadron, sometimes called the 'circus', heralded the new order of things. Then it was noticed that some of the enemy craft were painted with great rings about their bodies. Later, nothing was too gaudy for the Huns. There were machines with green planes and yellow noses; silver planes with gold noses; khaki-coloured bodies with greenish-grey planes; red bodies with green wings; light blue bodies and red wings; every combination the Teutonic brain could conjure up.* **❞**

Bishop was to add later that the first time he fired upon the Albatros his gun jammed, but the second time the pilot put his aircraft into a vertical dive from which he recovered and landed. There were no witnesses to this engagement in the air or on the ground.

Accumulated as a total for all flying units on the Western Front, the greatest number of flying hours was devoted to aerial reconnaissance and observation. Such duties were vital in the Arras and Aisne offensives and part of the role performed by No. 60 Squadron was the denial of such capabilities to the enemy. Not all observation was conducted from powered aircraft, and balloons were often used for this work.

On April 5, balloon strafes were ordered and two days later Bishop went into the air during the evening to hunt balloons over the line at Ecourt St. Quentin. He took off alone at 5:10 pm and flew east to rendezvous with a German observation balloon that had been up for several hours. Circling it from a distance at 5,000 feet to get the best position for attack, Bishop was suddenly jumped by an Albatros which missed and flew on past.

On its tail in a trice, the young Canadian got off 15-20 rounds at 300 feet and followed the aircraft down as it went into a steep dive. Wheeling around, he saw the ground crew huriedly winching down the balloon and its occupant. Bishop went immediately into attack and, *66 I dived on the balloon which was then on the ground and opened fire at 800 feet, finishing my drum when approximately 50 feet above it. Nearly all of the bullets entered the balloon and black smoke was visible coming out of it in two places. 99*

As a result of the dive, the Nieuport's engine clogged and sputtered to a stop, leaving Bishop to quickly select a place to land. At a mere 15 feet the engine fired back into life and Bishop pulled away amid a hail of bullets from guns on the ground. For this extraordinary versatility and quickness of wit, Billy Bishop was awarded the Military Cross. Next day, he was caught in an even more furious action when Maj. Scott led a patrol of five Nieuports. The weather was poor, there were heavy clouds around, and it was snowing:

66 There is a click of the electric ignition switch, the propeller is given a sharp swing over, and the engine starts with a roar. Once or twice there is a cough, but pretty soon she is 'hitting' just right on every one of her multiple cylinders. It is all the mechanics can do to hold her back. Then the pilot throttles down to a very quiet little purr and signals to the attendants to draw away the chocks from under the wheels. Slowly you move forward under your own 'steam' and 'taxi' across the field rather bumpily, to head her into the wind. This accomplished, the throttle is opened wide, you rush forward with increasing speed, you feel the tail of the machine leave the ground, and then you go leaping into space.99

Combats in the Air

Squadron: No. 60	*Date: 8-4-17*
Type and No. of Aeroplane: Nieuport Scout A6769	*Time: 9:30 a.m.*
Armament: One Lewis gun	*Duty: o.p.*

Pilot: Lieut. W. A. Bishop   *Height: 10,000 ft*
Observer: None
Remarks on Hostile Machine: 1 Two-seater
                              1 Albatros Scout
                              1 Balloon
                              1 Albatros Scout
                              2 single seaters
                              2 Albatros Scouts
                              and 1 double seater

While on O.P. at 9:30 am, I dived after Major Scott on a two-seater, opening fire twice as he was already diving. Then I engaged a single seater. He flew away eastwards after I had fired 40 rounds at him. Tracers hit his machine in fuselage and planes.

I then dived at a balloon from 5,000 feet and drove it down to the ground. It did not smoke.

I climbed to 4,000 ft and engaged an Albatros scout, fired the remainder of my drums at him, dodged away and put a new drum on and engaged him again. After two bursts he dived vertically and was still in a nose dive when about 500 feet from the ground.

I then climbed to 10,000 feet, and 5 miles NE of Arras I engaged two single-seaters flying towards our lines. Three more machines were above and behind. I fired the remainder of the drum into the pair, one burst of 15 at one and the rest at the second. The former turned and flew away with his nose well down, the second went down in a spinning nose dive. My tracers hit him all around the pilot's seat and I think he must have been hit.

Then I climbed and got behind the other three about the vicinity of Vitry. I engaged them, and one, a double seater, went down in a nose dive, but I think partly under control. I engaged the remaining two and finished my third drum at them. They both flew away eastwards.

(Sgd) W. A. Bishop Lieut.

Large clouds apparently separated Lieut. Bishop from the rest of the patrol. It will be observed that this officer engaged 5 H.A. single handed at one period during this patrol.

Major Scott, O.C. No. 60 Squadron, RFC

Maj. Scott was keen to propose six kills for Bishop but only four were allowed by his superiors at Wing and Brigade Headquarters. One of his victims that day may have been

> *You climb in great wide circles above the aerodrome, rig up the wireless, send a few test signals, get back the correct responses, and arrange your maps, while the pilot, with one eye on his instruments and the other on familiar landmarks, sets sail for the German lines, gaining height all the while. On the way to the lines you pass over your battery and send wireless word that you are ready to 'carry on'. It is to be a day of 'counter-battery' work, which means that some of our batteries are going to 'do in' some of the Hun batteries. The modern guns of war are very temperamental and restless. They get tired of firing at infantry trenches and roads and things, and more often go to shooting at each other. In this you help them all you can.*

Wilhelm Frankl who commanded Jasta 4, one of four Jagdstaffeln that would from the end of June comprise Jagdgeschwader Nr. 1 under the command of Manfred von Richthofen. For nearly two weeks Bishop had a frustrating time, one shared by his squadron commander. The intensity of aerial activity over the Western Front was taking its toll of pilots and machines. Patrols went out every day, with Bishop taking to the air three times on April 14, without success.

The losses were mounting faster than replacements could be brought in. In three days No. 60 lost eight men and their aircraft and Maj. Scott was forced to halt operations until

Below
Seen in July 1916, this Nieuport scout is equipped with Le Prieur rockets, eight of which could be carried and fired electrically from the interplane struts.

replacements arrived. Bad weather also prevented activity and the Nieuport Bishop usually flew (B6769) was destroyed when 2nd/Lt. Kimbell was shot down while flying it.

After five days of inactivity, Bishop was up again during the morning of April 19 but saw no aircraft and returned without encounters. He was now flying Nieuport 17 B1566, an aircraft in which he would score 31 victories and share credit for one more over the next three months. He set the record for the highest number of aircraft claimed by a pilot flying the same aeroplane in the Royal Flying Corps. Next day, when he went out alone, Bishop's luck returned:

Capt. Bishop (right) links arms with Lt. Soden holding a small dog in this posed group photograph taken at Filescamp on July 22, 1917, when the Canadian ace was with No. 60 Squadron, RFC.

Combats in the Air

Squadron: No. 60
Type and No. of Aeroplane: Nieuport Scout B1566
Armament: One Lewis gun
Pilot: Lieut. W. A. Bishop
Observer: None
Locality: Biache Sheet 51B I.11
Remarks on Hostile Machine: 1 Two-seater

Date: 20-4-17
Time: 2:58 a.m.
Duty: H.A.
Height: 8,000 ft

I engaged a two-seater by getting under him and firing with my gun pulled down at a range of 10-20 yards. I fired about 10-15 rounds, then dived twice, firing from 100 yards range. I dived a third time, opening fire at 30 yards range, and, looking back, after passing, saw smoke was coming out around the pilot's seat. In a few seconds flames were visible and the machine fell in a volume of smoke. I fired 80 rounds in all.

(Sgd) W. A. Bishop Lieut.

Returning to the ground to refuel and rearm after shooting down the Aviatik two-seater, Bishop went out again leading C Flight but they found nothing and returned empty handed. It had been another example of Bishop's success when operating as an individual rather than a team member. In some ways he was no different than men like Albert Ball but whereas the latter engaged the enemy with a fury bordering on recklessness, Billy Bishop calculated the situation with less haste and adopted a planned strategy. Such tactics worked well two days later when he was credited with his 11th victory while on escort to Maj. Scott who, claims Bishop, had been dispatched by higher authority on a single-seat photographic reconnaissance flight.

Combats in the Air

Squadron: No. 60
Type and No. of Aeroplane: Nieuport Scout B1566
Armament: One Lewis gun
Pilot: Lieut. W. A. Bishop
Observer: None
Locality: Vis en Artois
Remarks on Hostile Machine: 5 single seaters, probably Albatros

Date: 22-4-17
Time: 11.20 a.m.
Duty: O.P.
Height: 8,000 ft

While leading an O.P. I dived to the assistance of Major Scott 2,000 ft below me. He was attacked by five single seaters. I fired 15 rounds at one and he dived steeply apparently damaged. I then attacked a second one from the flank and fired 20 rounds at him. Most of the bullets apparently hit the machine. He went down through the clouds apparently out of control.

(Sgd) W. A. Bishop Lieut.

The remainder of the O.P. dived but were too late to catch the H.A. who all went down vertically through the clouds. The second machine at which Lieut. Bishop fired he saw run into his tracers, as he was holding well in front and the H.A. was flying level.

Major Scott, O.C. No. 60 Squadron, RFC

Later that day, Bishop went out three more times. At 3:30 pm he saw and engaged five German scouts without success; his 6:15 pm and 7:30 pm sorties were uneventful. Of his morning activities, Bishop says that Major Scott was on a special photographic assignment at that time, but it would have been very unusual to place such duty upon the commanding officer of a fighter squadron. Some have claimed that such were the losses among two-seaters and even scouts that April that it was a method of ensuring important information was safely obtained by using a fast aeroplane and a single pilot.

It was more likely that Major Scott was playing decoy to entice German aircraft down to a fight, thus denying the enemy the use of fighters that would maul Allied reconnaissance and observation planes. This was, after all, the purpose of continued use of fighters. Developed at first as a more efficient way of destroying these valuable eyes of the Army, fighters were

66 There was joy in flying these later days in April when a tardy spring at last was beginning to assert itself. The hardness of the winter was passing and the earth at times was glorious to see. I remember one afternoon in particular when the whole world seemed beautiful. We were doing a patrol at two miles up about 6 o'clock. Underneath us a great battle was raging, and we could see it all in crisp clearness, several lines of white smoke telling just where our barrage shells were bursting. The ground all about the trenches and the battle-area was dark brown, where it had been churned up by the never-ceasing fire of the opposing artillery. On either side of the battle-zone could be seen the fields, the setting sun shining on them with the softest of tinted lights. Still farther back - on both sides - was the cultivated land. The little farms stood out in varying geometric designs, with different colours of soil and shades of green, according to what had been sown in them and the state of the coming crops. There was no mist at all, and one could see for miles and miles.99 quickly adopted by all sides as a tool for not only protecting otherwise vulnerable aircraft going about their daily duties for the artillery or the infantry, but also for shooting down the very machines that could threaten the escorting fighters and lower the defensive screen.

Much has been made of the way certain aces attacked only the plodding two-seaters rather than risk defeat by engaging single-seat fighters. It is a moot point whether it was the fighters' purpose to deny the enemy the use of observation planes or to shoot down the aircraft that can protect them. Some pilots went for the more vulnerable observation planes while others preferred to attack the scouts. Von Richthofen is a case in point. Most of his victims were flying observation planes. Much has also been written about the prowess of individual fighter pilots, as though only the bravest and the best built up their scores on scouts and single-seat fighters.

One of the most fantastic we had met had a scarlet body, a brown tail, reddish-brown planes, the enemy markings being white crosses on a bright green background. Some people thought the Germans had taken on these strange hues as a bit of spring camouflage; but they were just as visible or even more so in the startling colours they wore, and we put it down simply to the individual fancies of the enemy pilots.

The last word on this would probably have it that von Richthofen did more damage to the enemy by destroying aircraft and their crews as well as preventing valuable intelligence information from being retrieved and utilised. He also, indirectly, helped the war effort by destroying enemy aircraft whose production was particularly manpower heavy. Men like Bishop found a natural talent for attacking single-seaters. Next day, he got the chance to claim another double, but only after three flights during the morning when no engagements took place:

Combats in the Air

Squadron: No. 60	*Date: 23-4-17*
Type and No. of Aeroplane: Nieuport Scout B1566	*Time: 3.23-3.59*
Armament: One Lewis gun	*Duty: H.A.*
Pilot: Lieut. W. A. Bishop	*Height:*
Observer: None	
Locality: Monchy le Preux - Vitry	
Remarks on Hostile Machine: 1 two-seater	
1 two-seater	
2 Albatros scouts	

At 3.23 p.m. at 2,200 feet I attacked a two-seater doing wireless 3 miles east of Monchy le Preux, firing from a flank and above. My gun stopped and when I had remedied it I dived again and fired about 15 more shots at it. My gun stopped again and the H.A. escaped.

I then flew east toward Vitry and engaged another two-seater, firing at it from behind and above. After a short burst he seemed to be hit and dived. I dived after him, firing all the way. He landed in a field near Vitry and I finished the rest of my drum at him on the ground. So far as I could see neither pilot nor observer got out of the machine.

At 3.59 p.m. at 8,000 feet, in sheet 51A near 17 I went to the assistance of another Nieuport attacked by three Albatros scouts. I attacked from behind on the same level and took one of them by surprise. He fell out of control and as one of the other H.A. was diving steeply and the other flying away pursued by the Nieuport, I followed him down and saw him crash at 12.

(Sgd) W. A. Bishop Lieut.

Billy Bishop had now scored 14 1/2 victories, including the one on April 8 shared with Maj. Scott, all achieved within one month of scoring his first on March 25. To mark his success, his mechanics made for him a blue spinner to put on his Nieuport and the Army made him a Captain, while Maj. Scott put him in charge of C flight. The next week did not prove as fruitful, but he did bag a balloon on the 27th and a Halberstadt D.III on the 29th.

As related in his combat report on the latter, **❝While flying at 17,000 feet I saw H.A. 3,000 feet below me. I dived at him from the sun side, opening fire at 150 yards. I fired in bursts of 3's and after about 12 shots he went down in a spin. I followed and fired the remainder of my drum, with the exception of about 10 rounds, at him. At about 11,000 feet he burst into flames. I climbed again to 15,000 feet and dived at another single seater. He dived away and I fired about 30 shots at him with no apparent result. I then saw another H.A. on my own level. I climbed above him and dived from the sun, but he dived away before I could get within 400 yards. I fired the remainder of my drum from long range but could observe no result. ❞**

❝I wasn't taking any liberties. I flew as straight ahead as I could, climbing steadily all the time. But at last I felt I had to turn, and I tried a very slow, gradual one, not wanting to bank either too steeply or too little. They told me afterward I did some remarkable skidding on that turn, but I was blissfully ignorant of a little detail like that and went gaily on my way. I banked a little more on my next turn and didn't skid so much.❞

Bishop had been flying top cover for a gaggle of four Nieuport scouts protecting two-seat observation aircraft lower down. The repetitive nature of uneventful flights is well illustrated by the countless times Bishop went out, either on accompanied patrol or alone, without success. Such elusive game was difficult to find.

Even at the height of 'Bloody April', days passed without a single victory, although a pilot could fly a dozen times or more searching for the enemy. Then, on April 30, Bishop had numerous engagements not untypical of air fighting during that hectic month, experiencing the kind of rapid action that was to increasingly characterise action in the air war. Unfortunately, not all were lucky enough to achieve such positive results:

Combats in the Air

Squadron: No. 60	**Date: 30-4-17**
Type and No. of Aeroplane: Nieuport Scout B1566	**Time: 9.45-12.15**
Armament: One Lewis gun	
Duty: O.P.	
Pilot: Capt. W. A. Bishop M.C.	**Height:**
Observer: None	
Locality: Lens - Monchy le Preux - Wancourt	
Remarks on Hostile Machine: Two-seaters	
Halberstadt Scouts	

At 10.10 a.m. south of Lens at 10,000 feet. While leading O.P. dived at 1 H.A. and fired 15 rounds with no apparent result. H.A. dived away eastwards.

At 10.10 a.m. north of Lens at 11,000 feet. Climbed up to two two-seater H.A. on our side of the line. I fired at one from underneath, getting off 15 rounds. The wire cocking device caught in the slide and I returned to the aerodrome to adjust it.

At 11.08 a.m. south of Lens at 11,000 feet. Not having found the patrol I attacked three two-seaters doing artillery observation. I dived on the leader and fired 10 rounds at him. He dived away and flew under three Halberstadt scouts. I was 500 feet above these so I attacked them from above, firing 20 rounds. I then flew away, as they had almost reached my level.

At 11.15 a.m. south of Lens at 8,000 feet. The three H.A. doing artillery observation returned and I attacked them, firing 20 rounds into the second machine. He went into a spin and I turned and attacked the last machine. He dived away and I followed, finishing my drum into him. He continued diving eastwards. I could now see the second machine still in a spin and only about 1,000 feet from the ground. The last one evidently landed as he did not come back.

At 11.25 a.m. east of Monchy at 6,000 feet. I attacked from above five Halberstadt scouts, who were flying as if to attack B.E.'s. I dived at them three times and fired in all about 20 rounds. They flew away east.

At 11.30 a.m. east of Wancourt at 5,000 feet. I attacked two machines doing artillery observation, firing at the rear one. They flew away east. I followed them to Vitry and again opened fire with no result. They came back to east of Monchy and I again attacked, finishing my drum into one.

At 11.45 a.m. north of Monchy. I attacked one of the above pair,

*firing at him head on. He flew away east losing height and neither
of them came back.*

*At 12.08 p.m. south of Lens at 11,000 feet. I dived on one H.A. doing
artillery observation and fired about 60 rounds, finishing my last
drum. He dived away east and landed about Sheet 360 V19 in a field.*

(Sgd) W. A. Bishop Capt.

What Billy Bishop reported as Halberstadt scouts were in fact
Albatros C.III two-seaters. They were the most prolific of all the
general purpose aircraft built by Albatros and could carry
either a light bomb load or operate as observation and artillery
spotting aircraft. But it was results and not positive identification
that counted in the air war, and Maj. Scott was so impressed by
Bishop that he wrote a glowing report to his superiors,
"recommending Captain Bishop for some recognition or reward.

"I beg now to suggest to you that the subsequent conduct of this
officer merits further distinction. On different dates between
the 6th and 30th April he has destroyed 10 hostile aeroplanes
and 2 balloons, while he has driven down 10 other German
machines. In the same period he has 34 times engaged enemy
machines. He often flies six or seven hours a day, two or three
hours by himself looking for hostile aircraft. Comment is, I
think, needless on this record of 24 days work, as the figures
seem to speak for themselves.

"One observation, however, I wish to add. By his gaiety and
gallantry, and in particular by his example in treating the
business of hunting H.A. as a sport, Captain Bishop has done a
great deal to induce other pilots to regard this pursuit from the
same angle. Where pilots have adopted this view the effect has
been to enormously improve the quality of their work, they then
find it very much less tiring."

Exaggeration creeps in to the report from Maj. Scott but this is
not uncommon in field commanders, and the Battle of Britain in
1940 is a classic example of how sincere people seeking honest
analysis can grossly over-estimate the performance of a unit and
even of individuals in combat. Nevertheless, testimony from
fellow pilots certifies the accuracy of Maj. Scott's remark that
Billy Bishop was a very lighthearted and thoroughly positive
asset to No. 60 Squadron. Out again twice on May 1 leading
patrols, Bishop was unable to find foe close enough to enagage
but on the next day a double again came his way:

Combats in the Air

Squadron: No. 60   *Date: 2-5-17*
Type and No. of Aeroplane: Nieuport Scout B1566   *Time: 9.50 a.m.*
Armament: One Lewis gun   *Duty: O.P.*
Pilot: Capt. W. A. Bishop M.C.   *Height:*
Observer: None
Locality: S. of Henin Lietard
Remarks on Hostile Machine: 1 single-seater
                             1 two-seater
                             1 two-seater

At 9.50 a.m. at 13,000 feet north-east of Monchy. While returning from photography escort I attacked one single-seater H.A. and fired two bursts of 5 rounds each. I was unable to catch him, and evidently did not hit him.

At 10.10 a.m. I saw five H.A. at about 6,000 feet doing artillery observation. I manoeuvred to catch one party of three when just west of the Drocourt-Queant line, as that was the nearest they were coming to our lines. I attacked the rear one and after one burst of 15 rounds he fell out of control and crashed near V1 or 2 just east of the Drocourt-Queant line. While I was watching him another two-seater came up under me and opened fire. I attacked him, firing about 40 rounds. He fell out of control and I followed 1,500 feet, finishing my drum. He was in a spinning nose dive and my shots could be seen entering all around the pilot's and observer's seats. Three more H.A. being above me I returned.

(Sgd) W. A. Bishop Capt.

Bishop had taken off at 9:00 am and was out until 10:40 am, going off again less than an hour later for almost two hours. Taking off at 11:35 am, he engaged a single-seat scout at 12:15 pm which he forced to land, bringing to three his log for the day. Other aircraft were attacked at 12:35 pm, 12:40 pm and 1:05 pm, but without success. Bishop was back on the ground at 1:20 pm and about 1 hour 45 minutes later he went up a third time, attacking German aircraft again at 3:45 pm and 4:30 pm without achieving a successful result. Such was the intensity with which he flew and fought. The next day he went up again for three patrols but nothing came his way; then on May 4, during the second of three patrols that day, he shared a victory with Lt. Fry.

Combats in the Air

Squadron: No. 60   *Date: 4-5-17*
Type and No. of Aeroplane: Nieuport Scouts   *Time: 1.15-2.00*
                            B1566 and B1597

Armament: Lewis guns
Pilot: Capt. W. A. Bishop M.C.
Lieut W. M. Fry
Observer: None
Locality: Brebieres
Remarks on Hostile Machine: 2 two-seaters

Duty: H.A.
Height: 5,500 ft

With Lieut. Fry following me I dived at two two-seaters. I fired 20 rounds at one end and turned off, Lieut. Fry diving on it and firing. I dived again as he stopped firing and fired about 40 rounds in the course of which the observer stopped firing. The machine did two turns of a spin and then nose dived to earth, where we saw him crash. I fired a short burst at long range at the second, which flew away and did not return.

(Sgd) W. A. Bishop Capt.

I dived with Capt. Bishop and fired a long burst at close range at the same time as him. The H.A. spun and crashed west of Brebieres.

(Sgd) W. M. Fry Lieut.

Lt. Fry had had to make an emergency landing two days before when the starboard wing of his Nieuport broke shortly after he had forced an Albatros to land. It was the second of only two shared victories in Billy Bishop's log of German aircraft and balloons destroyed, the previous one being the victory shared with Maj. Scott on April 8. After two patrols on May 5 and a day off on May 6, he was back in action the following day at 7:20 am when he took off for a forty minute sortie. Returning with his flight he set off alone at 9:15 am and pulled slowly to an altitude of 13,000 feet.

So quickly stated, these ascents to operational altitude gave much time for observing the presence of other aircraft in the air. It took Bishop almost twenty minutes to reach this height. Once there, he positioned himself with the sun behind him to remain hidden from approaching enemy aircraft. Almost immediately he spotted an Albatros D.III which he attacked at great speed and from very close range over Vitry. It fell away pouring smoke, and although Bishop was unable to see it land or crash he was credited with the kill as his 24th official victory.

Back on the ground at 10:15 am, Bishop took to the air for the third time that day at 2:00 pm with a patrol flying defensive cover for some F.E. two-seaters. A general melee ensued on the arrival of some Albatros scouts and one of them, a D.III, went down to Bishop's gun. It was the last patrol of the day. Bishop was going on leave for two weeks but just in case he could add to his score he got in a quick flight the following morning, taking off at 7.40 a.m. It was the first leave he had been able to take since joining No. 60 Sqdn, and it was not taken by choice.

In becoming a fighter pilot Bishop had found exactly what he wanted to do during the war and was thoroughly enjoying life. Yet for all his success, his meteoric rise so far was but a prelude for greater things to come. Ever mindful of the odds against his own survival, Bishop now received the gloomy news that Albert Ball had been shot down and killed that day, May 7, 1917. For long a personal hero and a model for Bishop's aspirations, Ball's legacy was a score of 44 confirmed victories.

CHAPTER FOUR *Aces High*

Leave from the Western Front was not always the pleasant digression from the harsh realities of war it was supposed to be. Locked into a constant cycle of rest, work and play, soldiers and airmen were given, or gave themselves, little time to ponder their situation. When relieved of that stress, other anxieties invaded the mind and body. It was no different for Billy Bishop, who so loved the opportunity to fly and fight. By his own word, he considered it a game.

Quick witted, cunning, and with a keen eye and certainly much bravery, Billy Bishop had the war he came to find: action, fun, frivolity and the chance to not only excel but to receive recognition from his superiors for his achievements. He stayed with Lady St. Helier in London and fully shared the hectic social life that surrounded her. Here was a contrast indeed.

Although touched by air raids from aeroplanes and airships, England still basked in relative isolation from the direct horrors of war. The constant flow of the dying and the wounded from battlefields all over the Western Front, the Middle East and Africa was a bitter lesson to those who thought, as most did in 1914, that it was to be glorious war.

The people of Great Britain were fast coming to realise that there is no glory in war, only sacrifice: if not of body, then of mind and spirit. But they could not truly feel the agonies their sons, brothers and fathers experienced daily on foreign soil, and everyday life went on largely unchanged. For those who could relieve themselves of the minor tedium of occasional air raids and war work through social functions and tea parties, it was a relatively acceptable irritant. The contrast seemed poignant to Billy Bishop, whose life had become a daily scrap high above the fields of France.

At first uneasy in this atmosphere of social parties and gaiety, he soon began to enjoy what to him had been another world of wealth and riches. Billy was a plain lad, accustomed to using his fists in a tight corner, imbued with a sense of self preservation. He had lived a largely unplanned life, taking opportunities as they came, and he was not quite at home in a planned, ordered environment where people could conduct their lives with precision and a level of predictability he had never imagined. Yet with each passing day Billy Bishop looked forward to returning to Filescamp and his boisterous, irreverent life at No. 60 Squadron.

In his absence, the usual round of duties had kept the squadron occupied, punctuated on May 19 by the sudden and unexpected arrival of a German aeroplane flying right over the airfield. In his haste to get off in pursuit, one pilot tried to take off with the chocks still under the wheels, his Nieuport doing a snappy somersault over the wooden blocks! Another pilot was better organised and quickly became airborne, but the German disappeared in cloud. Twenty minutes later he was found and Ltn. Georg Noth of Jasta Boelcke was forced to land and taken prisoner.

Jasta Boelcke had been formed as Jasta 2 in late August 1916. Led by the great air ace, Oswald Boelcke, it took the name of its first commander when he was killed two months later. Back with his squadron on May 22, Billy Bishop was in the air again three days later, ready for battle. Starting out at 8:35 am on May 25, he was up for less than an hour. Failing to see any aircraft he returned, to take off again at 11:25.

" Hunting the Huns had taken on a new interest at this time because suddenly their machines had appeared painted in the most grotesque fashion. It was as if they had suddenly got an idea from the old Chinese custom of painting and adorning warriors so as to frighten the enemy. We learned afterward that it was just a case of the spring fancies of the German airmen running riot with livid colour-effects. We wanted to paint our machines, too, but our budding notions were frowned upon by the higher officers of the Corps. But every day our pilots were bringing home fresh stories of the fantastic German creations they had encountered in the skies. Some of them were real harlequins of the air, outrivalling the gayest feathered birds that had winged their way north with the spring."

“ During the changeable days of the Arras offensive we had many exciting adventures with the weather. On one occasion I had gone back to the aircraft depot to bring to the front a new machine. Sunshine and snow-squalls were chasing each other in a seemingly endless procession. On the ground the wind was howling along at about fifty miles an hour. I arrived at the depot at 9 o'clock in the morning, but waited about until four in the afternoon before the weather appeared to be settling down to something like a safe and sane basis.”

This time there were aircraft about and five German scouts were seen; but they were too far away to catch and a third patrol during the evening brought no better luck. Bad luck too for Lt. Fry who had on May 2 landed after his lower wing broke. This time he had to make a hasty descent to No. 12 Squadron's airfield at Wagonlieu just west of Arras when once again the lower wing on his Nieuport broke. A weakness of the sesquiplane design, the Nieuport was prone to structural failure.

When Albatros copied the sesquiplane arrangement for its D.III scout it inherited this same tendency to failure and it was some time before the Germans correctly assessed the cause of the problem. The top scoring German ace, Manfred von Richthofen, nearly lost his life when the lower wing cracked in flight. Next day, Bishop scored his first victory since returning to duty, the first since receiving the Distinguished Service Order:

Combats in the Air

Squadron: No. 60	*Date: 26-5-1917*
Type and No. of Aeroplane: Nieuport Scout B1566	*Time: 09.35-10.40*
Armament: Lewis guns	*Duty: H.A.*
Pilot: Capt. W. A. Bishop D.S.O., M.C.	*Height:*
Observer: None	
Locality:	
Remarks on Hostile Machine: 1 single seater	
1 single seater	

At 10.04 a.m. over Lens at 9,000 feet. I dived on to one H.A. and fired 30 rounds. My tracers seemed to hit his centre section. I 'zoomed' and after turning was unable to find him again.

At 10.16 a.m. near Izel les Epeurchin at 11,500 feet. I attacked one H.A., being the highest and rear machine of a formation of six. I fired 25 rounds from underneath at 50 yards range with my gun down. The tracers went in his machine under the pilot's seat and the H.A. fell completely out of control in a spin.

(Sgd) W. A. Bishop Capt.

Along with C Flight, Bishop took off at 8:00 am on the morning of May 27 to head in the direction of Monchy. Climbing to around 3,000 feet and skirting the cloud base he caught sight of six German aircraft and led the attack. Again his gun jammed, and the cocking device failed. Returning quickly to the ground he dropped in at Wagonlieu to have No. 12 Squadron's mechanics repair it before he took off at 9.10 am to rejoin the fight.

Left
Although modified in fuselage design and structure, the Type 17 was a successful development of the Type 16, providing increased wing area and better handling characteristics.

By this time the scrap was over but Bishop caught sight of a German two-seater over Lens and went off in pursuit, only to be chased himself by two single-seat scouts. Pulling away in an apparent feint he drew out of range until they flew off, then caught up with the two-seater and destroyed it. Within minutes he attacked two fighters, possibly the ones he shook off earlier, putting bullets through one of them as it spun away.

Turning to attack the other one that quickly made off, he climbed to 16,000 feet and from that vantage point spotted another enemy aircraft below. Just at the crucial moment of attack his gun jammed and he was forced to break off the encounter and return to his airfield. He took off again at noon but was unable to find any more foe close enough to tackle. Nevertheless, combining the events of his first two patrols, the day's combat report looked good:

Combats in the Air

Squadron: No. 60
Type and No. of Aeroplane: Nieuport Scout B1566
Armament: Lewis guns
Pilot: Capt. W. A. Bishop D.S.O., M.C.
Observer: None
Locality:

Date: 27-5-1917
Time: 8.25-10.05
Duty: H.A.
Height:

At 8.25 a.m. east of Monchy at 3,000 feet. I dived on six H.A., the patrol coming after me. I fired 15 rounds into one and my gun jammed (cocking device). I fired a green light and left the patrol.

At 9.20 a.m. over Lens at 8,000 feet. I attacked a two-seater from behind and opened fire on him three times without apparent result. I was then driven off by two scouts.

At 9.40 a.m. over Dourges at 9,000 feet. I attacked the same two-seater and opened fire at 50 yards range. He immediately went into a spin and crashed in the village at Sheet 36C P14.

At 9.50 a.m. east of Lens at 11,500 feet. I attacked two scouts and opened fire at long range on one. He went into a spin and recovered 2,000 feet lower and flew away. The other climbed and I could not catch him.

(Sgd) W. A. Bishop Capt.

Early next morning the squadron commander, Maj. Scott, was out alone when he ran across a group of enemy aircraft which scattered at the first attack. Unseen by Maj. Scott, a group of S.E.5s from No. 56 Sqdn had been positioning to attack the German aircraft, and his action initiated a general dog-fight. During the course of this action a stray bullet struck Maj. Scott's fuel tank and forced him down to the ground. Landing only just inside the Allied lines he requisitioned a horse and rode to the nearest road to await a squadron car ordered by field telephone.

Rushing back to Filescamp, he arrived only just in time to receive the day's guest: General Allenby, General Officer Commanding Third Army, along with Scott's Brigade Commander and Wing Commander. Scott's dishevelled appearance was impossible to disguise but testified to the pace of air action along the Western Front. After three flights without success on May 28, Bishop was back in the air on the 30th and although five aircraft were sighted and engaged, once again his gun jammed and he was forced to pull away.

Luck improved next day when he got an Abatros D.V. *"I dived from the sun at the back of one of two H.A. firing about 10 rounds from 50 yards range. He turned and manoeuvred with me for a few seconds. I finally succeeded in getting another burst of 15 rounds in and he went down out of control."* Later, Bishop was to recall that his opponent was clearly an experienced pilot and that the fight lasted several minutes. For the final burst that caused the German to fall, Bishop claimed he got to within 45 feet of the Albatros scout.

Billy Bishop was yearning to increase his personal score and to do so with victories achieved by innovative means. His airfield

attack plan, carefully nursed in his mind since the casual chat with Albert Ball, would not go away. Thinking that better success would be achieved with at least two pilots he went around the squadron trying to recruit volunteers to his plan, but without success. Once roused from their slumbers in a dawn raid, the Germans would be no mean foe and Bishop had felt it would help to have a comrade alongside for defensive cover.

On June 1 Bishop flew three patrols in the morning and one during the late evening, returning as it was getting dark. That night there was a party in the mess and Bishop tried for the last time to get support for his daring airfield attack. Next morning, awakened at 3:00 am, he got dressed and took off precisely 57 minutes later. Back at 5:40 am, Billy Bishop had carried out his lone raid and would be awarded the Victoria Cross for extreme bravery and meritorious achievement in the face of great danger.

On each of the following two days Bishop carried out three patrols, frequently saw enemy aircraft and pursued several, but no fights ensued. On June 7 the squadron lost another pilot to structural failure when 2nd/Lt. Roland Harris was flying air-to-ground firing practice and both starboard wings on his Nieuport collapsed, sending his aircraft into a vertical dive. Maj. Scott immediately had himself helped into the cockpit of his Nieuport, whereupon he took off and continued the firing practice in an effort to restore confidence in the little biplane.

An effort was made to prevent this wing failure by attaching an additional flying wire to the upper wing. It was generally believed that the primary cause of the failure was the use of unseasoned Canadian spruce in the spars and ribs. That day Billy Bishop was out twice without effect but on the 8th he took to the air at 11:15 am and scored again, bringing his victory log to 32 kills.

Combats in the Air

Squadron: No. 60
Type and No. of Aeroplane: Nieuport Scout B1566
Armament: Lewis guns
Pilot: Capt. W. A. Bishop D.S.O., M.C.
Observer: None
Locality: Various
Remarks on Hostile Machine: Albatros scouts and two-seaters

Date: 8-6-17
Time: Various
Duty: H.A.
Height: Various

11.40 a.m. north-east of Lens 8,000 feet. I attacked a two-seater, firing two bursts in the course of three dives at him. He dived east. The observer stopped firing, either through being hit or his gun jammed.

11.52 a.m. south-west of Lille at 9,000 feet. I attacked a two-seater, firing 20 rounds at 200 yards range. He flew east.

12.10 p.m. 4 miles north of Lille at 11,500 feet. I attacked the two top machines in a larger formation of six scouts. I got on the tail of one and fired the remainder of my drum, about 45 rounds at him. He fell out of control. I watched him and he kept spinning all the way down and seemed to go straight into the ground.

12.17 p.m. at 9,000 feet. I dived at four scouts, firing short bursts from above at the rear machine. They flew away and I was unable to keep up with them.

(Sgd) W. A. Bishop Capt.

Below

A captured Nieuport in April/May, 1917, during the Battle of Arras. Although by this time well aware of its design characteristics, it gave the Germans another chance to study the aircraft.

For more than two weeks Bishop kept up his regular schedule of patrols in unsuccessful efforts to find enemy aircraft to attack. On the 9th he was forced to land at No. 12 Squadron's airfield when the cowling on his Nieuport broke. Three days later some aircraft were seen and chased but they were too far away. On the 13th the patrol saw eight enemy planes and again went in pursuit

but the Germans ran away. On the 15th Bishop went out with fifteen Nieuports of No. 60 Sqdn, desperately seeking a fight.

As one pilot commented, "We must have looked like a bunch of berserk eagles. We should have charged the Huns admission!" Some aircraft were attacked and one pilot did shoot down a yellow Albatros but the air action had subsided on that sector as the main action in the land battle had moved north.'

In an attempt to more precisely counter the German two-seat observation aircraft and prevent them reporting back to the artillery positions, the British 13th Wing had developed an Aeroplane Intercepting Station. By taking the bearing of wireless messages from the observation aircraft it was possible to plot via Aeroplane Compass Stations the location of these aerial observation posts. The squadron would assign pilots in pairs to stand by for instructions and then send them off in pursuit. Unfortunately, the enemy aircraft usually saw the British coming and ran away, only to return when they had gone.

This was frustrating work and the highly organised and command-orientated nature of the operation ran counter to the free-wheeling spirit of most fighter pilots, who preferred to operate within their own constraints. The endless patrols endured by the spirited young pilots in search of adventure were tolerable only because there was always a chance that the enemy might happen by. Some time later, Lt. Fry would recall with affection the days when Billy Bishop led his fledglings to the fray:

"Although I had lived and flown with Bishop as my flight commander during the previous two months I had never really got to know him or make friends with him - but then I found it difficult to make friends. He was very popular in the squadron, yet I do not remember him having any particular friends. He was a good-looking extrovert to a degree and took the lead in every off-duty activity.

"When it was time to turn back (after an early morning patrol), Bishop often gave a signal for the formation to break up when we crossed the lines and pilots could make their own way home independently. He and I and perhaps 'Nigger' Horn and others would lose all our height over the lines, come right down to nearly ground level over Arras and then hedge-hop all the way back to the aerodrome.

"We could see soldiers in the rest and reserve areas starting their day, with smoke rising from field kitchens or temporary cook-houses and were ourselves looking forward to breakfast.

&& From Arras I could see the Channel, and it resembled more a river of liquid gold than a sea. Across the Channel it was possible to make out England and the Isle of Wight. The chalk cliffs of Dover formed a white frame for one side of the splendid picture. Toward Germany one could see a tremendous wooded country, a stretch of watered lowlands beyond the trees, and the rest indistinct. To the south I could make out a bit of the River Seine, while to the north lay the Belgian coast. The marvellous beauty of it all made the war seem impossible. We flew peacefully along for miles in the full enjoyment of it all, and I shall always be glad we did not have a fight that evening. It would have brought me back to stern reality with too sudden a jerk.&&

When we arrived at the aerodrome we flew across it full out at ground level, zoomed up and landed off a turn. The C.O. was always on the aerodrome to ask how we had got on. I remember those mornings as being very happy, except when we had lost anyone on patrol, and to be quite honest, we did not let that worry us too much. It would have served no purpose."

On June 24 Bishop was up at 4.00 am but although sighting six aircraft he failed to reach them. Just over three hours after landing he was in the air once more, accompanied this time by three other pilots. Sighting a lone Albatros D.III in a tussle with three Sopwith Triplanes, Bishop led his Nieuports to their assistance but the German had out-manoeuvred the Sopwiths by the time he got there.

In spite of superior odds, the British were unable to get the better of this German pilot who Bishop later said had *exceptional quality. He managed to get into the middle of us, and it was all we could do to keep from colliding as we attacked him. Finally to add to our disgust he broke off the combat of his own sweet will just at the moment he felt he had had enough, and dived away. As we followed, diving after him, he would turn under us, then dive again, and repeat this performance. It was a most trying thing.*

After landing at 10:20 am Bishop was back in the air at 11:00 am heading north of Beaumont. Twenty-five minutes later he was at 12,500 feet and in pursuit of two Albatros scouts.
I attacked two enemy aircraft approaching the top one from behind and underneath. I opened fire from 20 yards range, firing about 20 rounds diagonally through his fuselage. He burst into flames and fell out of control. I then attacked the other enemy aircraft who was climbing up to me. I dived twice on him, firing about 25 rounds in all. He dived away through the clouds.

At 11.36 am west of Douai at 13,000 feet, I dived four times on three enemy aircraft, finishing my drum without result. I then flew away and they all flew east. Unsatisfied with the day's action, he was out again at 7:05 pm for more than an hour, but all was quiet in the air on that part of the Western Front. After a successful attack on a large formation of German scouts on the 25th when Bishop drove one Albatros down out of control, he scored another double on the 26th. *I attacked three scouts protecting one two-seater, surprising the top one. After 25 rounds he burst into flames and went down.*

One of the other two scouts dived down to the two-seater machine, the other turned and engaged me. I opened fire twice on

The squadron commander had been killed the day before I arrived from England, and the new one arrived the day after. It rather pleased and in a sense comforted me to know that the new commander was also going over in a single-seater for the first time when I did. He had been flying up to this time a two-seater machine which calls for entirely different tactics during a fight. Two-seater machines, as a rule, have guns that can be turned about in different positions. On the fighting scouts they generally are rigidly fixed. This means that it is necessary to aim the machine at anything you wish to fire at.

(Continued on page 81)

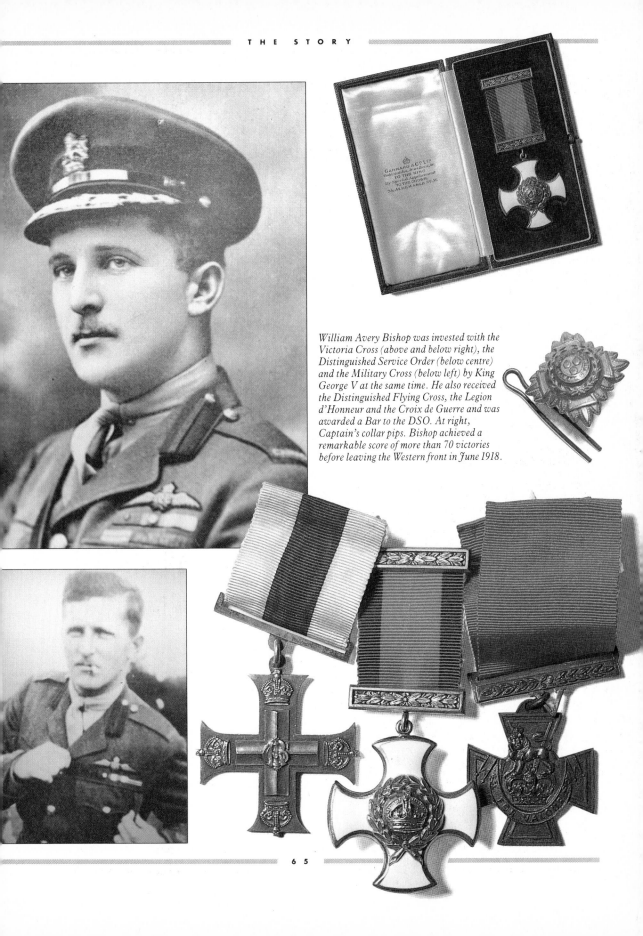

William Avery Bishop was invested with the Victoria Cross (above and below right), the Distinguished Service Order (below centre) and the Military Cross (below left) by King George V at the same time. He also received the Distinguished Flying Cross, the Legion d'Honneur and the Croix de Guerre and was awarded a Bar to the DSO. At right, Captain's collar pips. Bishop achieved a remarkable score of more than 70 victories before leaving the Western front in June 1918.

In the six years between attending the Royal Military College, Kingston, Ontario (far right), and commanding No. 85 Sqdn, RFC (below), Billy Bishop moved from obscurity to become a household name on two continents. Achieving recognition for his combat victories as a pilot and for bringing honour to his home country, the young Canadian is still remembered as a symbol of service and achievement. More than 70 years after he fought the Germans over the skies of northern France, Bishop is immortalised in books and films and his exploits have inspired the youth of two generations to fight for freedom in the skies over Europe. Bishop became a model for recruitment during the 1939-45 war and worked hard to generate support for the Royal Canadian Air Force.

Prior to leaving for England in 1915, Billy Bishop courted Margaret Burden (above) and proposed marriage shortly before leaving on a steamship to cross the Atlantic and join the war in Europe. Not before he returned from the war in 1918 were they to marry. The Bishops had three children, a baby that died at three weeks and a boy and a girl. His son, William Arthur, wrote a book about his father shortly after he died entitled The Courage of the early Morn, published in 1966.

Animals became mascots and pets for RFC squadrons on the Western Front and some were "captured" from local farms for dubious duties and a wide variety of pranks. Bishop cautiously leads the squadron's pet pig (left) which on at least one occasion was steered in the direction of a sleeping pilot officer, much to his dismay!

Billy Bishop achieved fame through his exploits claimed while flying a Nieuport 17 (B1566) which arrived at No. 60 Sqdn, RFC, on April 18, 1917 (left). It was also flown by Lt. W. B. Sherwood before being removed to St. Omer on August 17, 1917. There were other exponents of this diminutive French built sesquiplane, notably the British pilot Albert Ball who scored a total of 44 victories.

When Bishop went to war with the Royal Flying Corps he wore the single wing of an observer (above) until the attraction of piloting a single-seater made him into one of Canada's first fighter pilots.

"Nigger" in the arms of his master. The faithful dog was frequently seen with Bishop as well as other squadron members. When publicity photographs were commissioned, the dog had a field day and got in to many a rejected picture creating havoc among pilots and ground crew intent upon satisfying the demands of the photographer.

Overleaf

Bishop flies as an observer in the lumbering R.E.7, carrying out reconnaissance duties and dropping bombs on enemy positions. Developed from the R.E.5, this aircraft was dramatically underpowered and was incapable of carrying the loads for which it had been designed. Note the extended, unloaded, undercarriage legs hanging far below the fuselage. On landing the legs would telescope and assume their familiar length. Some measures were taken to improve the aircraft's lifting capacity and for a while the R.E.7 was put to use as an escort aircraft with the role of defending Allied bombers.

MICHAEL ROFFE

The accoutrements of a pilot's regalia in the Royal Flying Corps (near right) worn by Billy Bishop. The coveted wings were hard won in an age when training aircraft were frequently too old and poorly serviced, better aircraft being pressed into service in the war zone.

Although Bishop scored only 36 of his 79 possible victories in S.E.5 and S.E.5a aircraft (far right), he was to achieve higher daily averages in this aircraft than he did with the Nieuport which was his aircraft during the period when his fame grew quickest. The two aircraft were very different. The nimble Nieuport did not have the power of the S.E.5, while the latter had speed and twin machine guns to its advantage and became a well respected mount for the fighter pilot.

Exposed in open cockpits at high altitude, the RFC pilot of World War I was equipped with protective flying gear (below) including thick lined gloves and flying helmet with goggles. It was never enough to properly protect aircrew.

A vital piece of cockpit equipment was the compass (bottom picture), essential for maintaining course in good and bad weather. Taken from an S.E.5, this Air Compass Type 5/17 is typical in design. Directional flying was not a foregone conclusion when the war began and in the rush to produce operational aircraft the cockpit instrumentation sometimes left a lot to be desired. Very little feedback from the pilots and aircrew was evident and aircraft appeared at the Front with varying levels of finish and testing. One compass design had a horrible habit of swinging 180 degrees from true, to the consternation of all except the enemy.

Group Captain A. J. L. Scott, C.B., M.C., A.F.C. (right in picture above) commanded No. 60 Sqdn, RFC, between March and July, 1917, and was an important element in getting Billy Bishop's achievements recognised at higher level. With several famous air aces in his squadron, (then) Major Scott was a fascinating character in his own right, having come to flying from a successful legal career. Scott wrote his own book on the history of No. 60 Sqdn, shortly after the war, a lively and anecdotal history now available from Greenhill Books, Park House, 1 Russell Gardens, London NW11 9NN, England.

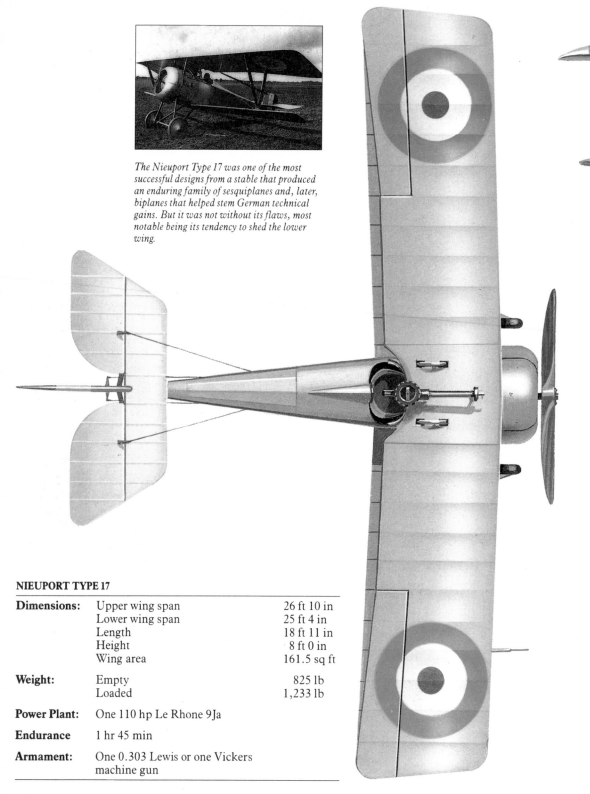

The Nieuport Type 17 was one of the most
successful designs from a stable that produced
an enduring family of sesquiplanes and, later,
biplanes that helped stem German technical
gains. But it was not without its flaws, most
notable being its tendency to shed the lower
wing.

NIEUPORT TYPE 17

Dimensions:	Upper wing span	26 ft 10 in
	Lower wing span	25 ft 4 in
	Length	18 ft 11 in
	Height	8 ft 0 in
	Wing area	161.5 sq ft
Weight:	Empty	825 lb
	Loaded	1,233 lb
Power Plant:	One 110 hp Le Rhone 9Ja	
Endurance	1 hr 45 min	
Armament:	One 0.303 Lewis or one Vickers machine gun	

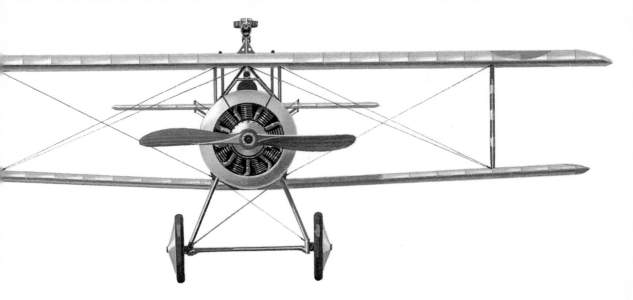

Bishop was one of two leading exponents of the Nieuport 17, the other being Albert Ball who flew this type for the first time when he was transferred to No. 11 Sqdn, RFC, on May 7, 1916. Aircraft were usually finished in aluminium dope although early models had olive drab. Flight letters were displayed in distinctive colours, as were aircraft numbers within the flight. These were displayed either side of the cockade – letter on one side, number on the other side – and on the top decking just behind the pilot. A Flight had red, B Flight yellow and C Flight blue. Bishop flew aircraft C5. The colour three-view shows the aircraft as it was when delivered to No. 60 Sqdn, RFC, in April, 1917. Later, Bishop had a blue spinner attached to B1566.

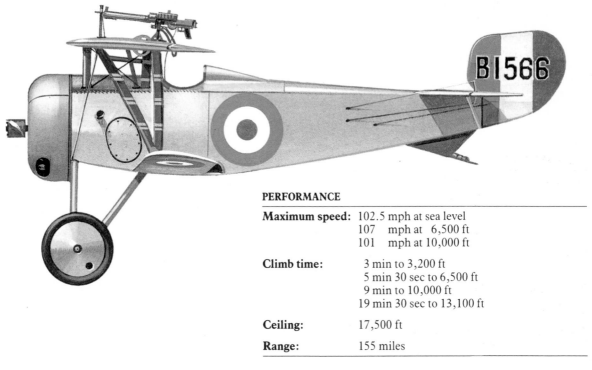

PERFORMANCE

Maximum speed:	102.5 mph at sea level
	107 mph at 6,500 ft
	101 mph at 10,000 ft
Climb time:	3 min to 3,200 ft
	5 min 30 sec to 6,500 ft
	9 min to 10,000 ft
	19 min 30 sec to 13,100 ft
Ceiling:	17,500 ft
Range:	155 miles

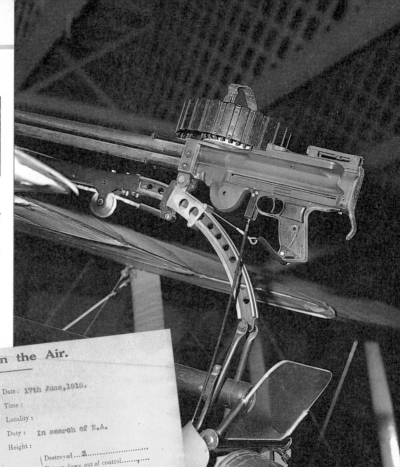

On performance alone the ageing Nieuport sesquiplane was surprisingly well matched against German aircraft like the Fokker Dr. I (above). As the Type 11, the sesquiplane first appeared more than two years before the triplane. Both types would soldier on through 1918.

Below, a typical combat report made out by Billy Bishop two days before his last fight in the air. In these three days he was to score 10 victories.

Combats in the Air.

Squadron : No.85

Date : 17th June,1918.

Type and No. of Aeroplane :
S.E.5A C1904

Time :

Locality :

Armament : 1 Vickers & 1 Lewis

Duty : In search of E.A.

Pilot : Major W.A.Bishop VC,DSO, MC.

Height :

Result
{ Destroyed ....2.................
{ Driven down out of control......,......
{ Driven down................................

Observer :

Remarks on Hostile Aircraft :—Type, armament, speed, etc.

Narrative.

10-25 a.m.   STADEN & HOOGLEDE.   18,000 feet.

(i)   Between STADEN & HOOGLEDE, 18,000 feet at 10-25 a.m. I turned back a two-seater who was approaching our lines, finally closing to 75 yards. After 20 rounds he burst into flames.

10-50 a.m.   SAILLY-SUR-LE-LYS.   4,000 feet.

(ii)   Over SAILLY-SUR-LE-LYS 4,000 feet at 10-50 a.m., seeing 1 Albatross I zoomed into the edge of a cloud. Albatross passed cloud & I secured position on tail. After 15 rounds he fell and crashed just south of village.

10-55 a.m.   LAVENTIE.(near)   2,000 feet.

(iii)   After attacking (ii) I saw a two-seater E.A. quite low, I dived at him from East but he turned and got East of me. After 2nd burst of 20 rounds he fell in a turning dive, then crashed between LAVENTIE and main road.

WA Bishop   Major,
Commanding..........Squadron.

A novel feature of the armament for Nieuport 17 scouts flown by the Royal Flying Corps was the Foster mounting, the idea of Sgt. Foster of No. 11 Sqdn. With this the pilot could pull the 0.303 Lewis gun back down toward the cockpit, elevating it for firing up into the belly of an enemy aircraft. Albert Ball was a seasoned practitioner of this method and inspired Bishop to follow the same tactic. When Ball went to the Royal Aircraft Factory to see the prototype S.E.5 he persuaded the designers to incorporate a Foster mounting in that aircraft (left). Note the telescopic sight along the forward fuselage.

The circular ammunition drum from a 0.303 Lewis machine gun showing top (right) and underside (left). Note the grab handle.

After Billy Bishop made his dawn raid June 2, 1917, on an unidentified German airfield (perhaps like that shown at left) he received the Victoria Cross and became a national hero. To this day, it has not been possible to positively identify which airfield he attacked.

Overleaf

A lone Nieuport 17 turns in to attack a German airfield several miles behind the lines. On the ground aircraft await action. Although Bishop claimed the aircraft he attacked were Albatros DI or DII with parallel interplane struts, it is possible they were Albatros DIII or DV pictured in this illustration by Mike Roffe. Airfield attacks were not uncommon and many heroic incidents like this were reported by RFC pilots in 1917 and 1918. Albert Ball provided the inspiration for Bishop's lone attack and after Ball was killed the Canadian pilot tried in vain to recruit support for his effort from fellow pilots. Bishop went out on one of his scheduled rest days and came back claiming three victories. His Nieuport was riddled with bullet holes and he was lucky to return alive.

The distinctive radiator of the Wolseley Viper engine (above) is seen to good effect. Note the busy cockpit interior (left).

One of the most outstanding aircraft of World War I was the S.E.5 (main picture) designed by the Royal Aircraft Factory in 1916. This particular aircraft carries the distinctive markings of No. 60 Sqdn, RFC, with engine cowling, lower wing root fairings, fin and diagonal fuselage band finished in the yellow of B Flight (see three-view notes) edged in white. Flown by Capt K. Caldwell, A8898 had been completed on April 18, 1917, before delivery to No. 56 Sqdn on May 1 and then via Marquis to No. 60 Sqdn on August 10, 1917. Just 16 days later RFC HQ issued orders that this marking was to be replaced by a single white disc positioned aft of the fuselage cockade and repeated, as a smaller disc, on the top of the fuselage aft of the cockpit. Bishop's aircraft (A8936) had sported red, white and blue rings around the nose.

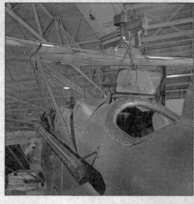

Displayed in the Royal Air Force Museum, Hendon, England, this surviving S.E.5a (originally F937 but changed in 1968 to F938) was one of the famous civilian skywriting aircraft (G-EBIC) of the 1920s, in which activity its fuselage was switched with the original F938.

In posed publicity shot taken shortly after his airfield attack of June 2, 1917, Billy Bishop shows how the Lewis gun is pulled back down on the Foster mount. This also facilitated ammunition drum changes in flight. Left, Bishop returns to Canada in 1918, his wife Margaret to his left. For Bishop, air combat was now a thing of the past but the record of his exploits would follow him. In World War II he would rally young Canadians to fight Nazi Germany. His son would become a Spitfire pilot after receiving his wings from his father and serve with No. 401 Squadron, RAF.

*him, the second time he went down completely out of control. I
continued firing until my drum was finished. I then flew away and
climbed 1,000 feet and dived at the scout and two-seater, firing 60
rounds at the latter from long range in two dives, with no
apparent result.* "

Despite two more patrols on June 27 Bishop had no luck, but the
next day he took off at 10:45 am into rain filled skies and climbed to
11,000 feet. " *Seeing four enemy aircraft under the clouds I
climbed above them and dived through hoping to surprise the
enemy aircraft. When 150 yards away the top one saw me and
turned. I fired on him from 100 yards range and my tracers seemed
to hit around his engine. The enemy aircraft put his nose down
turning sharply. I turned a moment later and saw the aircraft 500
feet under me, both of his left hand planes having come off, he was
falling vertically.* "

For several days Bishop was absent from patrol duty but on July 7
he was back in the air for his usual three patrols. But while routine
and uneventful for Bishop, his commanding officer returned from
leave with the news that he was to be promoted to Lieutenant
Colonel and given command of 11 Wing. Maj. Scott had
commanded an efficient squadron and was well liked by his officers
and men. He would be missed, especially by Bishop, but such is the
nature of service life, particularly during wartime.

Determined to get in as much flying as possible, Maj. Scott
stepped up his participation in patrols and on July 10 went up with
Bishop and several other pilots when alerted to enemy aircraft
reportedly attacking troops near Monchy-le-Preux. As Bishop
related later that day in his combat report, " *I led the patrol,
diving on seven scouts. I opened fire six or seven times, firing
bursts of about 15 rounds from ranges varying from 15 to
200 yards.*

" *One scout at which I fired 15 rounds at 15 yards range went
down completely out of control in a spin. I was unable to watch
him owing to other combats, athough I saw him still spinning
about 3,000 feet under us. During the combat Major Scott engaged
an enemy aircraft who was opening fire on me from close range.
Later the patrol dived on two scouts, who dived to the ground.* "
Major Scott, in fact, had intervened to save Bishop's life and
probably did so as nineteen aircraft swarmed around each other.

While Bishop was attacking a green Albatros two more scouts fired
at him from opposite sides. Major Scott went to drive off the one
which looked most dangerous, and got involved in a fight which

*" Those were very queer days. For a time it
seemed that both armies - German and
British alike - had simply dissolved.
Skirmishes were the order of the day on the
ground and in the air. The grim, fixed lines
of battle had vanished for the time being,
and the Germans were falling back to their
famous Hindenburg positions."*

left him wounded in the arm and his aircraft virtually shot to pieces. Only just managing to get back down on the ground, and with blood pouring down his arm, Maj. Scott was taken to hospital at Izy-le-Hameau.

His place as commanding officer of No. 60 Sqdn would soon be taken by Major 'Pat' Cochrane-Patrick, M.C. who, considered by Trenchard to be Britain's finest pilot, was very soon to receive a Bar to his M.C. and the D.S.O. for services during his stay at No. 23 Squadron. Two days later, on July 12, Bishop went up at 5:30 am for the first patrol of the day and went after a two-seat Aviatik photographic reconnaissance aircraft hovering 19,500 feet above sea level. Suffering from intense cold and diminished oxygen intake he was unable to control his Nieuport properly and fell toward the ground in a spin, recovering at lower altitude.

Like nearly all other pilots who come face to face with a Hun in the air for the first time, I could hardly realise that these were real, live, hostile machines. I was fascinated by them and wanted to circle about and have a good look at them. The German Albatros machines are perfect beauties to look upon. Their swept-back planes give them more of a bird-like appearance than any other machines flying on the Western Front. Their splendid, graceful lines lend to them an effect of power and flying ability far beyond what they really possess. After your first few experiences with enemy machines at fairly close quarters you have very little trouble distinguishing them in the future. You learn to sense their presence, and to know their nationality long before you can make out the crosses on the planes.

Later, at 12:25 pm, he took off for the second patrol of the day and shot down an Albatros D.III which crashed near Vitry. The fight involved No. 8 (Naval) Squadron and the renowned Australian pilot Flt. Lt. R. A. Little who had also achieved more than 30 victories in air combat. Little followed Bishop back to Filescamp and the two exchanged confirmation of each other's victory. After several more days of uneventful and routine patrols, Bishop secured two victories on July 17, which became his 40th and 41st kills.

Combats in the Air

Squadron: No. 60	Date: 17-7-17
Type and No. of Aeroplane: Nieuport Scout B1566	Time:
Armament: Lewis guns	Duty: E.A.
Pilot: Capt. W. A. Bishop D.S.O., M.C.	Height:
Observer: None	
Locality:	
Remarks on Hostile Machine: 2 enemy aircraft	
2 enemy aircraft	

13,000 feet, 3 miles north east of Havrincourt Wood. 7.43 p.m. I attacked two enemy aircraft, one being on my own level and one 600 feet underneath. I fired three bursts into one, the last burst he dived vertically and burst into flames 500 feet lower. The other enemy aircraft dived away.

10,000 feet, Marquion. 7.55 p.m. I joined in a fight which the Bristol Fighters were having and fired on two enemy aircraft. One enemy aircraft after two bursts at close range commenced to spin and either the tailplane or the elevators fell away.

(Sgd) W. A. Bishop Capt.

The last victory Bishop would score while flying his Nieuport 17 B1566 was achieved at mid-day on July 20. The weather had been cloudy during the morning but cleared in the afternoon. Bishop took off at 11:15 am and climbed to 13,000 feet over Havrincourt Wood. He saw three enemy aircraft and tried to creep up on them unnoticed but failed. Alerted to his presence they began to break formation and Bishop attacked the top aircraft, firing 40 rounds at it from between 150 yards and 50 yards range. The other aircraft broke off and Bishop pulled away from his victim to gain altitude but lost him in the climb.

Fifteen minutes later, just after noon, he caught sight of two more aircraft seven miles south east of Havrincourt Wood and into the rearmost one fired **" 15 rounds diagonally up from 30 yards range. He sideslipped, turned on his back and went down completely out of control. I dived on the second enemy aircraft, but was unable to catch him. I fired 20 rounds at him from long range. The first enemy aircraft I observed still out of control when it went through the clouds at 4,000 feet. "**

Bishop was up on patrol in his Nieuport every day until the 24th, when he carried out his last operational flight in this aircraft between 5:50 pm and 7:15 pm. The previous evening Bishop had taken charge of his new aircraft, an S.E.5 bearing the serial number A8936. Apart from obvious improvements in performance, a top speed of around 120 mph versus 105 mph for his Nieuport, the aircraft had two guns. A single Lewis gun was mounted above the centre section of the upper wing on a fixed track and could be pulled down in flight to change ammunition drums. A fixed belt-fed Vickers gun mounted on the port side of the fuselage just in front of the cockpit was synchronised to fire through the propeller arc.

The new aircraft was certainly having more than its fair share of teething troubles and so far had only been operational with No. 56 Squadron. Some pilots positively disliked the aircraft, Albert Ball being one, but it was gradually improved and would achieve distinction in the S.E.5a version. Some of the first S.E.5s to arrive at No. 60 Sqdn had displayed engine trouble and pilots were ordered not to cross the lines for fear an aircraft of this type would have to make an emergency landing and fall into German hands.

Bishop flew three patrols in his S.E.5 on July 27, including one during the afternoon when he got a chance to fire his guns, albeit without result. Despite orders to the contrary he went rushing across the lines during morning patrol next day to attack three German aircraft. Two fled and the third eventually

" I have not to this day fully analysed my feelings in those moments of my first victory. I don't think I fully realised what it all meant. When I pulled my machine out of its own somewhat dangerous dive, I suddenly became conscious of the fact that I had not the slightest idea in the world where I was. I had lost all sense of direction and distance; nothing had mattered to me except the shooting down of that enemy scout with the big black crosses that I shall never forget."

Overleaf
This splendid view forward from the cockpit area of an S.E.5a clearly shows the semi-enclosed Vickers machine gun, synchronised to fire through the propeller arc.

went down in flames over Phalempin to give Bishop his 43rd victory. With cloudy conditions and thunderstorms around, Bishop and two other pilots went hunting on the 29th, making an early start.

Seeing a two-seater near Beaumont, and although wary of a trap, they went off in pursuit; as expected they were pounced upon by four Albatros scouts from Jasta 12. One S.E.5 suffered engine trouble after a fierce dog-fight and it went down in flames killing its pilot, Lt. Gunner. Three more enemy aircraft joined the fight, which left Bishop and Caldwell to fend off seven Albatros scouts. There being only so many aircraft that can attack a plane at one time, the threat lay more in the reserves waiting to take up the challenge as an enemy machine went down.

66 The fates had been so kind to me in my first fight in the air, that the next time I crossed the lines my squadron commander had designated me as patrol leader. I knew this was a difficult job, but it was not until after we started out that I knew HOW difficult. First of all, I seemed to be leading too fast; then the pace would become too slow. Some of the machines seemed too close to me, and some too far away. I wondered why it was that everyone should be flying so badly today except myself. As a matter of fact, if I had been leading properly, the other machines would have found it quite easy to keep in their assigned places.99

Bishop managed to shoot one down as Caldwell fired off at another. Then Caldwell's gun jammed and he was forced to try and shake them off, finally managing to do so just 80 feet above the ground. Fighting for height again he joined Bishop, who was thrashing around the sky trying to keep all the enemy scouts at a distance. Caldwell charged full tilt right through the middle of the pack, scattering the enemy in all directions. Thus free of their assailants, the two S.E.5s scurried back to Filescamp.

August came and with it a major offensive known variously as the Third Battle of Ypres or, simply, Passchendaele, which would struggle on through to November and provide a mechanism for a further half-million casualties. As pointless in its way as the Battle of the Somme in 1916, it was a lesson in how not to use artillery to excess, how not to pound and pulverise into a gun-sucking quagmire millions of acres of shell-pocked farm land, and, most important of all, how not to use troops as a battering ram against machine guns and barbed wire.

On August 5 Bishop got his next victim during an evening patrol, when he spotted eight Albatros scouts and went in hot pursuit. At full throttle he charged toward the leader of the pack and fired twenty rounds into his aircraft before turning away to attack another machine. The leader spun back and came up into Bishop's flight path from behind. Suddenly, the enemy plane exploded in a ball of white fire close by two other machines of Bishop's patrol, momentarily shocking them into inaction. The aircraft went down as if lit by a flaming cauldron that observers on the ground twenty miles away could see clearly against the evening sky. Swinging round without pause, Bishop tore into another German aircraft and gunned it down from 50 yards with brief bursts of fire.

Next day he downed an Albatros D.V in an engagement that began at 10,000 feet between Quiery la Motte and Vis en Artois. *" Seeing three enemy aircraft below me I flew over a cloud and using it as a cover attacked by diving through. I fired on two without result. Suspecting a trap I then zoomed through the clouds and saw three enemy aircraft diving down apparently to attack me. I dived after them firing 40 rounds at the rear one. He dived vertically and flew straight into the ground crashing one mile north west of Brebieres.*

" I then left the fight, changed a drum, and returned with a Bristol Fighter carrying on a running fight with four of the remainder for 15 minutes with no decisive result. " Following a brief flight on August 8 when the sky seemed too empty to make it worthwhile staying aloft, Bishop conducted a patrol lasting one hour during the early morning of the 9th.

Combats in the Air

Squadron: No. 60	Date: 9-8-17
Type and No. of Aeroplane: S.E.5 A8936	Time: 8.45-9.00
Armament: 1 Lewis and 1 Vickers	Duty: E.A.
Pilot: Capt. W. A. Bishop D.S.O., M.C.	Height:
Observer: None	
Locality: See below	

8.45 a.m. north of Vitry at 10,000 feet. I attacked a scout, firing three bursts in all of 10 rounds each. He was a skilful pilot and I was unable to get a good sight on him. Finally he went into a spin which appeared to be controlled. I dived vertically but overshot him and he turned away. I then dived towards him, whereupon he went into another spin before I opened fire and continued through the clouds, when I lost him.

At 9 a.m. Havrincourt Wood, 14,000 feet. I saw a two-seater this side of the line. I climbed up to him, and when a mile from him he put his nose down and recrossed the line. I followed and overhauled him. The observer was firing all the time and I kept under his tailplane, waiting for his gun to jamb or run out of ammunition. Finally I got within 75 yards of him and opened fire. He fell completely out of control and finally spun and crashed into a field north of Ecourt-St. Quentin. The fight and chase had taken us from 14,000 feet to 6,000 feet. The pilot seemed afraid to put his nose down to more than 130 mph.

(Sgd) W. A. Bishop Capt.

" Seeing the modern war-aeroplanes riding through howling storms reminds one that it was not so long ago that a ten-mile breeze would upset all flying-plans for a day at any aerodrome or exhibition field. Now nothing short of a hurricane can keep the machines on the ground. As far as the ability to make good weather of it is concerned, the airman of today can laugh at a gale and fairly take a nap sitting on a forty-mile wind. "

With almost fifty aerial victories to his credit, Billy Bishop had risen to the crest of a self-made wave. His energy, drive, boyish enthusiasm for the chase and his unflagging spirit for adventure and excitement seemed undimmed by the violence and horror of death and destruction meted out almost daily from the twin guns of the biplane. Now came the crowning glory. News arived at Filescamp that he had been awarded the Victoria Cross for his lone airfield attack on June 2 with the credited destruction of three German aircraft.

It was time for celebration. Not just any party, but a major event chosen to be held on a day when clouds filled the sky and flying was put aside awhile. It started at Filescamp but quickly spread far and wide to other squadrons in the surrounding area. Alcohol flowed freely and unceasingly, fuelling the 'torchlighters' who seemed hell bent on rushing around letting off the Very lights used as signals on the ground and in the air. Had German aircraft been around they would have seen the place lit like a fairground.

66 The pilot who did not return was reported missing for about two months, and then we heard he had been killed outright, shot dead in the air. Upon looking back on this fight now, in the light of my later experience, I wonder that any of us got out of it alive. Every circumstance was against us, and the formation we ran into was made up of the best Hun pilots then in the air. They fought under as favourable conditions as they could have wished, and one can only wonder how they missed completely wiping us out.99

Then a genuine torchlight parade began which set off from Filescamp and invaded every village and hamlet within staggering distance. Soon, the entire front was awash with news and rumours of the big celebration. Brigadier General Higgins, General Officer Commanding IIIrd Brigade, was seen sailing horizontally through a mess window only to recover himself, stagger back and send the perpetrator the same way through the same window. Champagne and wine flowed and reinforcements arrived, in the form of suppliers and consumers, from squadrons and RFC units several miles away.

As the revelry and merry-making grew in intensity mess floors, bars and tables were awash with alcoholic drinks of dubious mixture, fuelling a ribald sing-song. Someone got on a piano and every time he missed a note a bottle went flying through the air in his general direction. Taking to the road, the party invaded huts, tore tents to pieces, dismantled the mess and drove all manner of animal life from their nocturnal resting places. Friendly banter gave way to pushing and shoving, uniforms were ripped off and a general wrestling match got under way.

As the night wore on the earliest to indulge began to fall by the wayside and at dawn the airfield was littered with the sleeping remnants from No. 60 Sqdn as well as several other units. A precise chronicle of Bishop's participation in this celebration has mercifully never been recorded but testimony indicates that he was an active participant in all scheduled and unscheduled events!

On the 11th Bishop made two flights, one during the morning and the second during the early evening. Poor weather cut the morning flight to 25 minutes while the evening flight lasted 90 minutes, but without result. The following day he received the citation to his V.C. linking it to the airfield attack on June 2. Bishop was up again during the afternoon of August 12 but no enemy aircraft were seen. Several were, however, encountered during a flight in the evening but without success.

For some time now Billy Bishop had known he was about to leave No. 60 Sqdn. He had been told he was to be transferred to an Air Fighting School and, keen to obtain as many victories as possible, he sought every opportunity to fly and to fight. On August 13 he took off at 6:35 pm and climbed through low clouds on his way to a double victory.

Combats in the Air

Squadron: No. 60	*Date: 13-8-1917*
Type and No. of Aeroplane: S.E.5 A8936	*Time: 7.2 pm*
Armament: 1 Lewis and 1 Vickers	*Duty: D.O.P.*
Pilot: Capt. W. A. Bishop V.C., D.S.O., M.C.	*Height: 11,000 ft*

Observer: None
Locality: 5 miles south of Douai
Remarks on Hostile Machines: 3 Albatros scouts

While flying above the clouds I saw three enemy aircraft slightly above me. They had seen me first and the leader attacked, outdistancing the other two. I turned and approached head on. At 300 yards I opened fire and he immediately swerved. I continued firing and passed quite close to him. On looking over my shoulder I saw him burst into flames and dive. One of the others then attacked, the third one shooting from 500 yards at the same time at me. I manoeuvred with the second one and fired a burst, then managed to get on his tail. At 50 yards I opened fire. He burst into flames after about 20 rounds and fell in a spin. The third enemy aircraft escaped. I dived through the clouds after him but he was then too far away to catch. The other two were still falling ablaze.

(Sgd) W. A. Bishop Capt.

A thunderstorm on the 14th kept Bishop away from possible attacks on German aircraft, such as there were in the air that day, but his luck returned again on the 15th. Taking off at 7:55 pm he climbed up through 11,000 feet penetrating patchy cloud most of the way before sighting three enemy aircraft flying toward the east. Approaching the one at the rear, Bishop opened fire with his guns, firing thirty rounds from each, and watched

"It was a German boast at this time that their retreat from the Somme had upset the offensive plans of the British and French for months to come. How untrue this was they were soon to know. We Canadians knew that the first big 'push' of the spring was to come at Vimy Ridge, where the Canadian Corps had been holding the line grimly the entire winter through. It had been a trying ordeal for our men, who were almost at the foot of the ridge with the Germans everywhere above them."

as the aircraft tumbled over into a spiral and fell 8,000 feet
before the murk of the evening light folded around the falling
speck and it was lost to view. Next day, Bishop took off at 6:25
pm in fine weather and scattered clouds. It was to bring him his
last two victories for more than nine months.

Combats in the Air

Squadron: No. 60
Type and No. of Aeroplane: S.E.5 A8936
Armament: 1 Lewis and 1 Vickers
Pilot: Capt. W. A. Bishop V.C., D.S.O., M.C.
Observer: None
Locality: see below

Date: 16-8-1917
Time: below
Duty: E.A.
Height: below

At 7.3 p.m. 14,000 feet over Harnes.

*While chasing two scouts I saw a two-seater approaching the lines
slightly above me. I put my nose up and fired a short burst. He
immediately turned and I closed in underneath firing. He did a turn
and a spin and two planes fell off, a moment later the planes on the
other side fell off.*

At 7.6 p.m. at 13,000 feet over Carvin.
*I chased two scouts which were approaching and turned away,
firing at the rear one at long range. He went into a spin after
80 rounds and I watched him crash half a mile north of Carvin.
The other enemy aircraft escaped.*

(Sgd) W. A. Bishop Capt.

In five months Billy Bishop had accounted for one third of all
the aircraft shot down by No. 60 Squadron and in doing so
inspired the young pilots to greater efforts, brought great credit
to the squadron and became the envy of many aspiring fighter
pilots. Now he was going back to England and his squadron was
going to Ste. Marie Cappel. It would soon be in the thick of the
Battle of Passchendaele Ridge and would take part in ground
attack missions carrying four small 25-pound Cooper bombs
under each S.E.5 and S.E.5a.

Bishop would be well out of it, but his mind would ceaselessly
wander back to Filescamp and the sheer exhilarating fun of
dashing through the skies, of laughter and fun in the mess and
of the comradeship that links men about to die. There was a
touch of this nostalgia when he said goodbye to the squadron.
**❝When I left the aerodrome to start for England I had a vague
feeling I would not be back. I had heard nothing more about my**

transfer, but the very fact that there was a great deal of uncertainty made me anxious, and I remember, when leaving the old place, turning round to have a last look at it. **"**

CHAPTER FIVE *An Ace Supreme*

It was very different this time. Now Billy Bishop was a hero and a national celebrity the public wanted to see, applaud and decorate. What better place to start than to have the King publicly recognise the nation's feelings by decorating him with the Victoria Cross, the Distinguished Service Order and the Military Cross at the same time. The King had never done that and it was an important 'first' for a nation that increasingly sought unique ways both to justify the war and to garner public support for further recruitment.

The giant threshing machines of death and destruction could not be adequately fed from the volunteer force alone. Kitchener's Army was insufficient to supply the men the war effort needed. They were being killed and maimed too quickly, and the nation had to gather up more effectively the young men technically eligible for service. Day-to-day life had already been affected in Britain. Women and children were put to work in munitions factories and from the age of thirteen children left school to join the ranks of those waiting to step into the factory shoes of men destined for France and Flanders.

By 1918 one-half the work force employed in aircraft manufacturing comprised women and children, and of the latter a considerable proportion were under thirteen years of age. Incentives were given to parents who allowed their less academic children to be 'relieved' of the stress extra school time brought on. In an age when the actions of young people were controlled to a greater and more mature age by their parents than in later generations, such things could be organised. Parents were encouraged to have children and young people move to relatives in towns and cities where munitions work was available. And more grotesque encouragements sought adoptions for children who could serve the war machine by moving from the country where job prospects were low.

By 1916 the need for more troops had been met through conscription and from March that year all men between the age of 18 and 40, later 45, then 50, years were called up. A plan existed in 1918 to raise the senior age to 60. From a Regular Army of 250,000 in 1914, the number of men provided from the United Kingdom by 1918 had risen to 5 million. Yet despite conscription there were still too few massing the ranks. The colonies and dominions of the British Empire were pressed to recruit more men. Heroes like Billy Bishop were important recruiting tools and were a focus for pride within the dominions. So it was that this most famous Canadian of the moment went to Buckingham Palace in August to meet King George V.

Bishop had been staying with Lady St. Helier at Portland Place and it was she who had prepared him for the special event, in addition to arranging social functions to mark the day and writing to his parents to keep them informed: "Billy is going to the investiture on Wednesday. While he feels rather nervous about it, being his first time, I am so glad he has not been before, because Princess Marie Louise told me last week that the King said the one thing he wanted was to give the V.C., D.S.O., and the M.C. at the same time, preferably to a Colonial officer and now Billy is the first person who has won them all and the King is very pleased as he has heard so much about him from the Princess. He is very well, although he looks a little older perhaps, and one would never believe all he has gone through."

To cap it all, Bishop was promoted to the rank of Major and given a Bar to his Distinguished Service Order in recognition of "great skill and gallantry." What mattered equally to Billy, however, was just what sort of job the Royal Flying Corps had in mind for him. He really wanted to go back to France. His personal score meant a lot to him and he had an eye on the several good pilots quietly logging victories on the Western Front. The round of parties, social events, award ceremonies and the universal recognition he received almost everywhere he went were enjoyable but Billy was an action man at heart and

We called the big, elongated gasbags 'sausages' and the French did likewise - 'saucisses'. They floated in the air at anywhere from 800 to 3,000 feet above the ground, and were held captive by cables. These cables were attached to some special kind of windlasses which could pull the balloons down in an incredibly short space of time. Sometimes they would disappear as if by witchcraft. Wherever the sausages flew they were protected from aeroplane attack by heavy batteries of anti-aircraft guns, and also by what we came to know as 'flaming onions'. These 'flaming onions' appear to consist of about ten balls of fire, and are shot from some kind of rocket gun. You can see them coming all the way from the ground, and they travel just too fast to make it possible to dodge them. I have never had an 'onion' nearer than 200 feet from me, but the effect of these balls of fire reaching for you is most terrifying, especially the first time you have the pleasure of making their acquaintance.

Left
Success came rapidly to Bishop and by June 1918 he was already marked down for a "political" role in helping to form the nascent Canadian Air Force.

having found his war he wanted to fight it. After all, it could not go on for ever!

Seeking out Lord Cecil at the War Office, Bishop enquired about his posting to the Air Fighting School in Scotland. Bishop had first learned of this possibility during his last few weeks at No. 60 Squadron. Work was still going on to make the place ready and Billy was discouraged from the expectation that he would soon be sent there. Higher authority had other things carved out for Billy Bishop and they were probably right to assume that only a return to combat would put his talents to their best use. Because he was such a notable figure, now the leading British air ace, only command of a squadron of his own would combine all the best options for his future career. But not just yet.

Once again, most probably with the help of Lady St. Helier, Billy was granted leave to return home until the end of the year, and he left England in early September aboard a troop ship bound for Canada. Arriving at Montreal by train he was met not only by his family but a representative selection of local officials, dignatories, press people and anyone else who wanted to be seen with the famous Billy Bishop. Four years of war, many dead and injured and very little to show for it was having its effect on morale. Bishop would be a valuable showpiece for the establishment in bolstering popular support for this far-off war in a far-off land.

As was customary in that period the press felt themselves to be guardians of the establishment and rallied to defend the

Below
Others on the Western Front had yet to achieve their greatest fame. One such man was Hermann Goering, seen here on the extreme right, chatting in front of a Fokker D.VII.

government. It had been that way in Britain, where the press contrived a way of hiding the true facts of the war from the general public and conspired together to keep their stories the same. Without radio and television, the general public had no other means of knowing what was going on. Consequently, Bishop was a popular subject for press coverage and his movements were keenly followed.

One event that produced the desired effect was Billy's marriage to Miss Margaret Burden on October 17 at the Timothy Eaton Memorial Church in Toronto. A mass of people lined the route from Margaret's home to the church and enthusiastically cheered the couple when they emerged as man and wife. After the fourth Christmas of the war, pleasantly more endurable for the Bishops than for most serving in the armed services that December, it was time to make preparations for a return to England early in the new year. This time Bishop was accompanied by Margaret and when he visited Lord Cecil in London he heard the news that he was to command a new squadron on the Western Front.

No. 85 Sqdn had been formed during August 1917 from the nucleus of C Flight at the Central Flying School, Upavon. Living variously first at Norwich then at Hounslow just outside London, the squadron was destined for Petite Synthe on the outskirts of Dunkirk in Belgium after three days at Marquise, north-east of Boulogne. Meanwhile, Bishop was given almost a free hand to choose his flight commanders and his pilots. By now the Americans were heavily involved in the war, the first air units having arrived in France during early September 1917. Until that time they had fought either in a special French unit of volunteer Americans or via Canada.

Bishop's flight commanders came from No. 60 Sqdn and elsewhere but all were men he knew and could trust. He also wanted three Americans who caught his eye, Elliot White Springs, who had more flying hours than any other pilot at his English training school, Larry Callaghan and John Grider. This, he was told, was impossible so Bishop went personally to U.S. Headquarters and began the process that would eventually oust bureaucracy and give him his three Americans. Billy did not want to get embroiled in the day to day administration any more than he had to and good men around him would relieve him of that burden. His eye was still on active combat flying and the opportunities for improving his score.

For a while, however, he was kept busy in England selecting personnel and working up No. 85, which was now a Royal Air

The British do not officially announce a hostile machine destroyed without strict verification. When you are fighting a formation of twenty or more Huns in a general melee, and one begins a downward spin, there is seldom time to disengage yourself and watch the machine complete its fatal plunge. You may be morally certain the Hun was entirely out of control and nothing could save him, but unless someone saw the crash, credit is given only for a machine driven down. The Royal Air Force is absolutely unperturbed when its losses on any one day exceed those of the enemy, for we philosophically regard this as the penalty necessarily entailed by our acting always on the offensive in the air.

Force squadron, since on April 1 the Royal Flying Corps and the Royal Naval Air Service had merged into the RAF. Somebody knew a Lord who rented a four bedroomed house to the squadron recruits. Elliot White Springs and John Grider recalled life in those weeks before France: "We moved in and gave a big dinner party Saturday. Major Bishop, Nigger Horn, MacGregor, MacDonald, Captain Benbow and Captain Baker came in from Hounslow for dinner...We found out too late that we couldn't get any meat without coupons. And there was little else we could buy. We got around the food problems easily.

"All we had cooked was soup and fish. Then we made a big tub full of (South Carolina) Eggnog and a couple of big pitchers of Mint Julep. To make sure that no-one got beyond the fish course we shook up cocktails too. Our guests arrived about six and we started doing bottoms up in rotation. It was a riot...At the end of the fish course I was alone at the table. The rest were chasing each other all over the place." The unlikely juxtaposition of Bishop and his irreverent friends with high society ladies and royalty, introduced into his life by Lady St. Helier, was a humorous mixture of the rough and the smooth.

As one participant would recall of events one day when they were invited to tea by Bishop's wife, "Mrs Bishop (who would soon be living with Lady St. Helier) had a lady with her and she invited us to tea with them. We explained that we were dirty, which we were, but she said never to mind and to come along as we were; so we did. We all went to the squadron office and had tea brought over from the mess. The lady with her proved to be very nice and was very interested in Americans and America. She was the most patriotic person I've met over here because she is always talking about the King.

"When I told her how much all the Americans liked serving with the British, she said she was so glad and she knew the King would be delighted to hear it. That sounded a bit far fetched to me. As we went out we saw Cunningham-Reid's mother nearly break a leg curtseying and I noticed Mrs Bishop doing the same thing when we left her and took the lady out to the bus. I asked Cunningham-Reid why the gymnastics and he told me it was...Princess Marie Louise. All three of us have been trying to remember whether we cracked any jokes about the King or not. Mrs Bishop must have been laughing merrily. She's a peach."

On May 22 the squadron left for France to a great fanfare and a full assembly of various girlfriends, wives, the Princess Marie Louise and an assortment of high ranking British and American officers including Colonel William (Billy) Mitchell. First stop

Technically, the Germans seldom gave a machine 'missing', for the fighting is practically always over their territory, and every one of their machines driven down can be accounted for, even if it is totally destroyed. Many of our losses are due wholly to the fact that we have to 'carry on' over German territory. Any slight accident or injury that compels a descent in Hunland naturally means the total loss of the British machine. But such a loss does not involve a German victory in combat; it is merely a misfortune for us. If the machine could only have reached our side of the lines it might have been repaired in half an hour. The public often forgets these things when reading of British machines that fail to return.

Far left
S.E.5a s of No. 85 Sqdn, RFC, with Billy Bishop's aircraft in the foreground. Note the squadron marking aft of the cockade and the individual letter forward.

was Marquise before arriving at Petite Synthe three days later. In the months since Bishop had been in France the war had changed. There was a balance at work and it was tipping, ever so slowly, in favour of the Allies. Not by anything they had done but through circumstances no-one could accurately predict nor any one person control.

The Allies had gained the Americans, who theoretically went to war with Germany in April 1917, but had in fact been helping the Allies for years. It took a while for manpower and arms production to gear up in the country that had been established to rid itself of European squabbles; but 1918 was seen by the Allied and Central Powers alike as the year when the full weight of American resources would lean upon the Germans. So much so that the Germans instituted the Amerika Program, whereby their fighter squadrons would double, and other increases in air strength would compensate for the new forces.

Every class of our machines was now engaged in the preparations for the big offensive. The bombing squadrons were out by day and by night. They would fly over the lines with only the stars to guide them and drop tons of high-explosive wherever it was considered that the resulting damage would have a crippling effect upon the defensive power of the German machine. Our photographers were busy during every hour of sunlight, and our artillery observing machines were keeping long hours in company with the guns, carrying on the preliminary bombardments.

The Germans had gained the use of troops previously massed on the Eastern Front by the virtual capitulation of Russian forces. The Treaty of Brest Litovsk, signed in March 1918, ended three months of an armistice which had sealed large tracts of land into the provenance of the German Empire. Riddled throughout with unease and potential revolt, the workers of the new Russia had, however, inspired German soldiers to question the status quo. There were deep murmurings in the ranks, as indeed there were in the ranks of Allies, although the latter would always veil that rising from public view.

It was clear to the Germans that they had one last chance, and that was to mobilise a giant push known variously as Operation Michael and the March Offensive. Horrified by what he saw happening in Europe, the American President Woodrow Wilson had made a dramatic call for peace on terms which would leave the combatant powers intact and stable. The Germans tore it up by the Treaty of Brest Litovsk and by the biggest battle of the war.

It started at 4:50 am on March 21 when forty-six German divisions got ready to attack the confluence of the British and French armies, and 6,100 German guns opened up along a front forty miles long; one large artillery piece every 45 feet. For two hours gas shells rained down, mixing an acrid yellow haze with a rising, early morning fog, followed by high explosives that pounded the Allied infantry. Buttressed by Operation Georgette, the second element of the offensive, the assault continued.

Within three weeks the Germans had advanced almost forty miles from St. Quentin to Mondidier, reaching almost as far west as Amiens. In five weeks the first phase was over and once again a great offensive became mired because of the defenders' stubborn refusal to yield ground. In those five awful weeks of ceaseless attack and counter-attack, the Allies and the Germans suffered 78,000 dead, 430,000 wounded and 330,000 taken prisoner. Unlike all the others, this offensive had a positive result. It shook up the stalemate and started Germany on the slippery road to defeat as it finally proved to the Central Powers that they could not win the war by military might. Faced with political and social decay it was only a matter of time before Germany caved in.

No. 85 Squadron arrived at Petite Synthe on May 25 and it took Bishop only two days to settle in and resume his victory log. This time he had an S.E.5a, serial number C6490. It was mid-afternoon on May 27 when he lifted cleanly into fine skies dotted with low clouds. Over Houthulst Forest across the German side of the lines he stalked a German two-seater, but tiny dots in the distance grew into German scouts and Bishop pulled back to the Allied side knowing the foe would not follow.

Increasing his altitude to 17,500 feet he cautiously worked his way back and found another two-seater which quickly turned tail and ran. Faster than the lumbering observation plane, Bishop caught it, fired a few rounds and saw the wings come away before it plummeted to earth. He was back with a vengeance to shoot down more German aircraft and defend his ascendency over other upcoming aces.

There were several. Bishop was no longer the top scoring British ace. Having exceeded in August 1917 the 44 aircraft shot down by Albert Ball, he had been away from the front long enough for James Byford McCudden to catch his score and overtake it, totting up 57 kills when he was retired to England in February. Bishop now had 49 single-handed victories and shared two with other pilots. McCudden would soon be back to increase his own score and an Irishman by the name of Mick Mannock was also building his tally.

It was becoming a race against time, and every day Bishop was well aware that an injury could put him out of action, or a spell of bad luck keep him lower down the ranks. Next day, May 28, Bishop took off during the early afternoon for his second patrol of the day, eagerly seeking a victim. An earlier patrol had provided only a frustrating chase after a fleeing two-seater that

"It was a strange thing to be skimming along just above the ground in enemy territory. From time to time I would come on groups of Huns who would attempt to fire on me with rifles and pistols, but I would dart at them and they would immediately scatter and run for cover. I flew so low that when I would come to a clump of trees I would have to pull my nose straight up toward the sky and 'zoom' over them. Most of the Germans were so startled to see me right in their midst, as it were, they either forgot to fire or fired so badly as to insure my absolute safety. Crossing the three lines of German trenches was not so comfortable, but by zigzagging and quick dodging I negotiated them safely and climbed away to our aerodrome. There I found that no bullets had passed very close to me, although my wing-tips were fairly perforated."

refused to stand its air space. Climbing to 15,000 feet Bishop headed in the direction of Ypres and circled. He saw a gaggle of scouts some 3,000 feet below and swooped to attack them, firing at two aircraft on the port side of the group. One, a Pfalz, went down in flames and the other fell away smoking, its fate unknown. He had scored his 50th solo victory.

Two days later Bishop increased his score by three victories, achieved in two patrols. Maintaining his preference for flying alone, and leaving his flight commanders to take out groups of aircraft, Bishop scored twice within three minutes in mid-afternoon, and again in the evening. His double consisted of two two-seaters which he reported as Albatros types while his third was an Albatros D.V which fell to earth from 15,400 feet over Armentieres. As with most of Billy Bishop's victories, there were no witnesses; the price paid by the lone warrior. Next day, Bishop accounted for three more and submitted two combat reports, one for each patrol in which he scored.

66 The next ten days were filled with incident. The enemy fighting machines would not come close to the lines, and there was very little doing in the way of aerial combats, especially as far as I was concerned, for I was devoting practically all of my time to flying low and helping the infantry. All of our pilots and observers were doing splendid work. Everywhere we were covering the forward movement of the infantry, keeping the troops advised of any enemy movements, and enabling the British artillery to shell every area where it appeared concentrations were taking place. Scores of counter-attacks were broken up before the Germans had fairly launched them. Our machines were everywhere behind the enemy lines.99

Combats in the Air

Squadron: No. 85   *Date: 31st May 1918*
Type and No. of Aeroplane: S.E.5a C/6490   *Time: 3.5 & 3.15 pm*
Armament: 1 Lewis and 1 Vickers   *Locality: Quesnoy &*
Pilot: Major W. A. Bishop V.C., D.S.O., M.C.   *Lille*
Observer: *Height:*
Destroyed:
Driven down out of control: 1
Driven down: 1

At 3-05 p.m. 14,000 ft over Quesnoy 5 miles north east of Armentieres

I attacked one of three Pfalz scouts sitting 2,000 feet above a formation of about fourteen enemy aircraft. I fired 20 rounds at 20 yards range from behind. Enemy aircraft immediately fell completely out of control. I was unable to watch it owing to presence of the remainder of the enemy aircraft formation.

At 3-15 p.m. 6 miles south west of Lille at 11,000 feet.

I attacked a two-seater enemy aircraft who was evidently an artillery observation machine. I fired a long burst from rear at 100 yards range, enemy aircraft turned to left, then dived east and landed in a field.

(Sgd) W. A. Bishop Major Commanding 85 Squadron.

Combats in the Air

Squadron: No. 85	*Date: 31st May 1918*
Type and No. of Aeroplane: S.E.5a C/6490	*Time: 8.15 pm*
Armament: 1 Lewis and 1 Vickers	*Locality: 2 mls N.*
Pilot: Major W. A. Bishop V.C., D.S.O., M.C. of Estaires	
Observer:	*Height: 11,000 ft*
Destroyed: 1	
Driven down out of control:	
Driven down:	

Seeing white Archies two miles east of Hazebrook I flew in that direction and saw one enemy aircraft scout underneath me near the A.A. burst. I dived at him but suddenly saw another enemy aircraft higher just re-crossing the enemy lines, followed him and fired 20 rounds from each gun at 50 yards range. Enemy aircraft fell to bits and fell 2 miles north of Estaires.

This enemy arcraft must have been seen by A.A. batteries of the 2nd Army as visibility was very good.

(Sgd) W. A. Bishop Major Commanding 85 Squadron.

Next day Bishop headed a flight of four aircraft which included the American, Springs. This airman was to become one of the most famous pilots from across the Atlantic, chronicling as a very accomplished author events of World War I and eventually becoming a highly successful businessman. After being shot down at the end of June he would be ordered to the American 148th Aero Squadron where he became their leading ace with 12 victories. But on the evening of June 1 he was still in pursuit of his first victim when Billy Bishop took his flight at full charge into six Pfalz scouts at 11,000 feet. Just minutes later four had been shot down.

❝We were acting, you might say, as air policemen. Occasionally one of our machines would be set upon by the German gangsters - they were 'careful' fighters and seldom attacked unless at odds of four to one - and naturally we suffered some casualties, just as the ordinary police force suffers casualties when it is doing patrol duty in an outlaw country. The weather was always favourable to the German methods of avoiding 'open-air' combats. Even the clearer days were marked by skies filled with clouds sufficiently large and dense enough to offer protection and hiding-places to the high winging Hun machines.❞

Combats in the Air

Squadron: No. 85	*Date: 1st June 1918*
Type and No. of Aeroplane: S.E.5a C/6490	*Time: 8-10 p.m.*
Armament: 1 Lewis and 1 Vickers	*Locality: La Gorgue*
Pilot: Major W. A. Bishop V.C., D.S.O., M.C.	
Observer: Height: 11,000 feet	
Destroyed: 1	
Driven down out of control:	
Driven down:	

While on practice patrol, I led patrol consisting of Captain Horn, Lieut. MacGregor, Lieut. Springs, diving on six enemy aircraft. I fired four bursts at one enemy aircraft, zoomed and dived again on to the leader's tail, fired 30 rounds from 50 yards, enemy aircraft went down in a straight dive, then spun and crashed near La Gorgue. During fight I saw Lieut. MacGregor shoot down enemy aircraft, which fell completely out of control a long way and another enemy aircraft fell completely out of control from above me. This must have been shot down by Lieut. Springs, I saw it still out of control quite low down. Lieut. MacGregor also shot down another enemy aircraft out of control. Lieut. Springs confirms the enemy aircraft I shot down.

(Sgd) W. A. Bishop Major Commanding 85 Squadron.

66 By this time I had learned nearly all of the fundamental principles of fighting in the air and had more or less decided upon exactly what tactics were best for me to use. I also realised the exact limit of my ability in carrying these various tactics out, and in fighting acted accordingly. I was more than ever firmly resolved now that, having got so far in the game and past its most dangerous stages, I would take no foolish risks, but continue to wait for the best opportunities. It was very hard to restrain oneself at times, but from the middle of May until I left France in August, I lost only one man out of my patrol killed, and he was shot down on an expedition when I was not with him.99

Although Bishop's duties were heavily concentrated upon working up his squadron ready for a move to a more operationally active area, he still found time to go out on lone scouting missions looking for aircraft to bag. He was out again during the evening of June 2 in fine weather but poor visibility. Flying over Armentieres again he saw and attacked a black Pfalz scout with a white tail, and shot it down.

The Pfalz scout had first appeared during mid-1917 and began to join Jagdstaffeln later in the year. It was a robust fighter, very slightly smaller than the Albatros D.V but with a performance almost to match it. With twin synchronised Spandau machine guns across the nose it was developed by Pfalz Flugzeugwerke when contracts to licence-build L.F.G. Roland D.II single seat scouts expired. This aircraft was seen increasingly over the Western Front as the lack of a new volume production fighter began to affect the Jagdstaffeln that faced the RAF fighter squadrons.

Only the Fokker D.VII showed promise of restoring German technical equality with new British fighters such as the Sopwith Camel and Dolphin and the soon to appear Snipe and Salamander. The Albatros had been around a long time and although large numbers were still in service the type was criticised by Manfred von Richthofen as early as mid-1917. Now it was too late to switch from volume production of second best aircraft, and the German scouts were increasingly vulnerable to better, faster and more robust Allied aircraft. The S.E.5a, was proving a particularly effective fighting aeroplane, especially in the hands of the initiated.

On June 4, after a day's respite, Bishop scored two victories against Albatros scouts flying in overcast skies. The patrol had been detailed as escort for a bombing raid on Zeebrugge. The aircraft assigned the bombing duty flew across at 12,000 feet, with the S.E.5as of No. 85 Sqdn 2,000 feet higher, flying top cover.

Combats in the Air

Squadron: No. 85
Type and No. of Aeroplane: S.E.5a C/6490
Armament: 1 Lewis and 1 Vickers
Pilot: Major W. A. Bishop V.C., D.S.O., M.C.
Observer: Height:
Destroyed: 1
Driven down out of control: 1
Driven down:

Date: 4th June 1918
Time:
Locality:

Time: 11.28 a.m. Locality: half-way between Nieuport and Ostend and 3 miles out to sea. Height: 14,000 feet.

Seeing a formation of eight enemy aircraft out to sea, I flew towards them from the east and diving, attacked a straggler, after 10 rounds from each gun, he burst into flames and fell burning brightly. I zoomed away and escaped.

Time: 11.37 a.m. Locality: Leffinghe.
Height: 15,000 feet.

I attacked another straggler of the same formation. Diving from the east on them and zooming away, fired 30 rounds from each gun at 75 yards range. Enemy aircraft which was a silver Albatros, fell completely out of control and passed through clouds 8,000 feet below still out of control.

66 *When flying alone or with just one other, it is always a case of constantly turning around in your seat, turning your machine to right or left, looking above and around or below you all the time. It is a very tiring piece of work, so it is but natural that when you have three or four other men behind you, you spend more time looking in the direction where you hope the enemy machines are, if you want to attack them, and to looking at any interesting sights which are on the ground.* **99**

(Sgd) W. A. Bishop Major Commanding 85 Squadron.

Poor weather moved across the English Channel and for several days the squadron was unable to get in its quota of flying. Life around the aerodrome was informal, to say the least. Bishop was not a disciplinarian and showed little enthusiasm for the usual 'spit and polish' of some other units. This comes across clearly in a letter written to a family friend, Emma Cox, from American John Grider.

"We had an awful raid night before last. One of the squadrons near here comes over in force. We repelled the attack with six gallons of Eggnog and, much to their chagrin and disgrace, had some of it left when they departed. Springs has been appointed DOC (Drinks Officer Commanding) and has a huge nickel-plated cocktail shaker that was made by the air mechanics in the squadron. He flew from England with it tied to one of his struts.

The mess was situated on the very edge of the aerodrome and about twenty yards from a farmhouse, which possessed the most extraordinary farmyard I have ever seen. There were pigeons by the hundreds, and all kinds of fowl possible to imagine. A small pond in the middle of the farmyard afforded exercise and amusement for a flock of ducks. The raising of pigs, however, seemed to be the farmer's great specialty, and to these pigs I owe many amusing hours.

One afternoon, while looking through the farmyard three of us decided to capture a large hog and trail it back to our quarters to shoo it into the room of a friend, who was at the moment sleeping. It was very easy to get the idea, but for inexperienced people it was a difficult job to get the porker.
After much mature deliberation we decided upon our victim - the largest and dirtiest one in the farmyard. We took the pig into the mess to show him about, putting him in a little cage made of the fire-fender. He seemed quite satisfied here for a moment, then, deciding that he would like to get away, stuck his nose under the edge of the fire-fender, heaved it over his back, and with a disgusted grunt walked out. Feeling that he had earned his freedom, we let him go.

"This is surely a wonderful bunch. I would like you to know them. They worry about nothing at all and our nights are a series of song and good cheer. We have a piano and a vitrola. It is a big family, there is no discipline. We have breakfast from eight to eleven and everyone is happy. Everybody is keen on the job; you are not afraid of being let down in a scrap."

The absence of discipline, the carefree way in which the patrols were conducted, and Bishop's predilection for rushing off on his own in search of German aircraft, leaving his fellow pilots to fend for themselves, had been noted by Wing Headquarters. Passed up and across to the War Office, it was decided that Billy Bishop should move aside for another commanding officer who could take on No. 85 and mould it into a tight, disciplined, fighting force. Bishop belonged to the old scool and there were fewer and fewer of them.

The RAF still needed men like Billy Bishop but it could not afford to let them loose in a pack of young, impressionable neophytes. Bishop had a lot of flying experience and had come up the hard way, first spending his time plodding across the lines in old reconnaissance and bombing aircraft, then learning to fly and eventually becoming a highly capable fighter pilot. He had nothing to regret but he was not able to bridge the very different roles of lone hunter and squadron commander.

Awaiting the call to move south to St. Omer, a distance of less

On one occasion we went over to photograph an aerodrome in the vicinity of Douai, a city you can see from the top of Vimy Ridge on any clear day. We had with us in all about twenty machines, and were a very formidable party indeed. As luck would have it, we spied two Germans. With two or three other of our fighting pilots, I quickly dodged to one side to try to engage the Huns before they could see the whole crowd of us and be frightned away. But, no luck! They made off the minute we turned our noses in their direction.

Right
Despite pressures on his time running operations at No. 85 Sqdn, Bishop was able to rapidly improve his score. But he was still the solo flyer and the lone fighter.

than twenty miles as an S.E.5a flies, the squadron was on stand-by and during mid-morning June 11 got the call to roll. The relaxed atmosphere was apparent. Some officers were still asleep. The transport arrived at noon and the squadron packed up and left on the rough road south. The pilots flew their aircraft down to St. Omer, a huge base through which so many squadrons had been routed as they arrived in France. From here, too, many squadrons would be sent to other airfields where they would hone their fighting capabilities before being dispatched to an operational sector.

Bishop was leaving and would shortly return to Canada. He had little time in which to increase his score. It was becoming clear that the war really might soon be over, perhaps by Christmas. The Germans were being pressed hard and pushed back toward their border. Morale was flagging in their ranks and rumours of capitulation spread. The Bolsheviks were working hard to convert German popular opinion in their favour and anarchy was breaking out in the country. Bishop lost no time in settling in at St. Omer and on June 15 he was back in action once more. Now he had a different aeroplane, C1904; Lt. Springs had accidentally rolled into Bishop's machine when returning from a lone flight and a particularly fierce scrap behind the lines.

As Bishop related in his combat report for that day, striking almost a record for brevity, **❝I attacked one of four enemy aircraft which were sitting above large formation of enemy aircraft. In course of combat I fired at three of the four, finally shooting one Pfalz down in flames from 50 yards range and behind. ❞** Bishop also noted on his report that the Pfalz had a red fuselage and black wings and that it had been accompanied by Albatros scouts.

The combat took place 3 miles east of Estaires at 17,500 feet. There now followed an intensive period of flying and fighting in the four days before he was to leave No. 85 Squadron. A period in which he was credited with twelve aircraft. The run began on June 16 when he took off during the evening into changeable weather.

❝ 'Nigger' was one of my own dogs. One night, returning after having dined with some other unit, I found 'Nigger' outside my hut. He was a big dog, looking very much like an Airedale, only black. It was pouring rain and very cold, so I took him in and let him sleep on my bed with me. He had a most affectionate way about him, and although quite the smelliest dog I have ever known, it was a pleasure to have him about.
The other dogs each had their good points. Rachel - who was a little deformed fox-terrier we had picked up on the road simply because she was the ugliest-looking thing we had ever seen - turned out to be a wonderful ratter, frequently taking on rats twice as long as she was, and, although getting badly bitten herself, she would invariably come out of the scrap victorious. Nobody would claim Rachel, but she got fed somehow, and also got quite a lot of attention, so she stayed with us.❞

Combats in the Air

Squadron: No. 85	*Date:16th June 1918*
Type and No. of Aeroplane: S.E.5a C1904	*Time:*
Armament: 1 Lewis and 1 Vickers	*Locality:*
Pilot: Major W. A. Bishop V.C., D.S.O., M.C.	
Observer:	*Height:*

Destroyed: 2
Driven down out of control:
Driven down:

At 8.20 p.m. 1,800 feet 5 miles east of Armentieres.

I chased a two-seater from our side of the lines climbing up to him finally geting to 100 yards range fired 20 rounds from each gun. Enemy aircraft smoked then burst into flames and fell.

At 8.28 p.m. 8,000 feet over Armentieres.

Four Albatros scouts attacked me from the sun and head on continued their dive to 4,000 feet below me. I watched for a few minutes and dived onto rear one, opened fire at 75 yards from behind and in the sun. Enemy aircraft went down vertically and crashed on western edge of Armentieres. Enemy aircraft dived to below me I think owing to presence of one of our formations three or four thousand feet above.

(Sgd) W. A. Bishop Major Commanding 85 Squadron.

❝ *In our home in a beautiful green orchard, our life was full of the most extraordinary contrasts. One minute we were as far removed from the war as if we were in South America, and an hour later we would be fighting for our lives or carrying on in some way directly connected with the mad world-struggle. It all added to the lure of life and somehow made the real fighting, when it came, seem less real and tragic.***❞**

There had been little opportunity for patrols during the day. The squadron was still settling in but Bishop was already counting the days to when he would leave and hand over to his successor. Inspired by the attraction of a final burst of activity he eagerly watched the skies for clearing weather. The forecast was not good for the next several days but come what may he had to do his utmost to raise his score. Capt. McCudden would be back on the Western Front in three weeks and Mick Mannock was closing fast on Bishop's total; the fiery Irishman now had 59 victories to his credit and many said his true score was much greater since he often attributed aircraft he shot down to novices as encouragement.

June 17, and thunderstorms were expected that afternoon. Bishop was out during the morning over the lines toward Hooglede after having climbed to 18,000 feet. When he returned to file his combat report, there were three more German aircraft to his credit.

Combats in the Air

Squadron: No. 85   *Date: 17th June 1918*
Type and No. of Aeroplane: S.E.5a C1904
Time:
Armament: 1 Lewis and 1 Vickers   *Locality:*
Pilot: Major W. A. Bishop V.C., D.S.O., M.C.

Observer: *Height:*
Destroyed: 3
Driven down out of control:
Driven down:

10.25 a.m. Staden and Hooglede. 18,000 feet.

(i) *Between Staden and Hooglede, 18,000 feet at 10.25 a.m.*
     I turned back a two seater who was approaching our lines,
     finally closing to 75 yards. After 220 rounds he burst into
     flames.

     10.50 a.m. Sailley-sur-le-Lys 4,000 feet

(ii) *Over Sailley-sur-le-Lys 4,000 feet at 10.50 a.m., seeing one*
     Albatros I zoomed into the edge of a cloud. Albatros passed
     cloud and I secured position on tail. After 15 rounds he fell and
     crashed just south of village.

10.55 a.m. Laventie (near) 2,000 feet

(iii) *After attacking (ii) I saw a two-seater enemy aircraft quite*
      low, I dived at him from east but he turned and got east of me.
      After second burst of 20 rounds he fell in a turning dive, then
      crashed between Laventie and main road.

(Sgd) W. A. Bishop Major Commanding 85 Squadron.

> *All of June was marked by the most perfect weather. The prevailing strong west winds stopped and a light breeze blew constantly from the east. Some days there was hardly a stir in the air. From dawn until sundown there was rarely a cloud in the sky, and although the heat-waves from the effect of the sun on the earth made flying very rough when near the ground, the days were wonderful, and we all felt like kings. The mornings were very busy, as there were many calls to chase away hostile aircraft; but the afternoons we generally had to ourselves, and although it was necessary to stay right on the aerodrome, we found many amusements there.*

On June 18 Captain Edward Mannock, D.S.O. and Bar, was promoted to Major and left No. 74 Squadron at Clairmarais North (north east of St. Omer) to go on leave. While he was in England he spent some time with McCudden, returning to France on July 5 to command No. 85 Squadron which Bishop left on June 19. Mannock would mould No. 85 into an efficient fighting force, dramatically raising their performance record and stamping upon them his own edicts. Four days later his friend McCudden was killed in an accident en route to join his new command - No. 60 Squadron, where Billy Bishop had achieved so many victories.

Enraged at this loss, Mick Mannock threw himself into a furious assault upon the enemy. Exactly three weeks after taking command of No. 85 Sqdn he had raised his personal victory score from 59 to 73, thus becoming the highest scoring British air ace of World War I. In reality there was probably a greater margin than the single official victory that separated him from

> *When I left for my leave to England, I was not very keen on going. The excitement of the chase had a tight hold on my heartstrings, and I felt that the only thing I wanted was to stay right at it and fight and fight and fight in the air. I don't think I was ever happier in my life. It seemed that I had found the one thing I loved above all others. To me it was not a business or a profession, but just a wonderful game. To bring down a machine did not seem to me to be killing a man; it was more as if I was just destroying a mechanical target, with no human being in it.*

Above
Always a popular figure, Billy Bishop had little time for discipline and ran a casual squadron. He was replaced briefly by Mick Mannock who forged a tight fighting unit that quickly achieved fame as a squadron.

Billy Bishop because only Mannock knew for sure just how many victories officially credited to others were rightfully attributable to his guns. Sadly, he was not awarded the Victoria Cross until almost exactly a year after his death on July 26, 1918.

Bishop's penultimate attempt to increase his score came on June 18. The weather had improved and there were fair skies although the afternoon was overcast. The squadron's casualties had been mounting over recent days and moods were sombre as the morning patrols were prepared. Bishop left for a lone patrol, intending to join up with the others later if nothing came his way. It was on that patrol that one of the most popular pilots in the squadron, Lt. John Grider, was downed and killed on the German side of the lines. Out with Lt. Springs, he became separated and nobody ever discovered the reason for his fall. But luck favoured Billy Bishop again that day.

Combats in the Air

Squadron: No. 85
Type and No. of Aeroplane: S.E.5a C1904
Armament: 1 Lewis and 1 Vickers
Pilot: Major W. A. Bishop V.C., D.S.O., M.C.
Observer:
Destroyed: 2
Driven down out of control:
Driven down:
Remarks on Hostile Aircraft: Albatros scouts,
natural wood fuselage

Date: 18th June 1918
Time: 10.45 a.m.
Locality: 6 mls NE

Height: 9,000 feet

While looking for one of the Squadron Patrols I saw four enemy aircraft scouts in a gap in the clouds circling around each other. I dived into the cloud and came out in the gap just above them, secured position on tail of one. After a very short burst, he seemed to explode and went down in flames. At the same moment one of the other three spun away, of the remaining two, one attacked me the other firing wildly from 300 yards on one side. I fired a long burst in a deflection shot at enemy aircraft fighting me, and he smoked then burst into flames. Fourth enemy aircraft then spun away and I fired 20 rounds at him with no result.

(Sgd) W. A. Bishop Major Commanding 85 Squadron.

It was some time before the fate of John Grider was known. No-one had seen him go down and there were no reports of an aircraft having been seen on the ground. For Bishop, it was not a happy way to leave his squadron. He was, however, leaving for political reasons over and above the need to give No. 85 Sqdn a more effective leader. Although by no means unanimous on the need for such a force, Bishop's countrymen were keen to develop a Canadian Air Force, for which he had pledged support. As their greatest air hero, Bishop was to play a leading role in organising the CAF. His last chance to score while he still had time on the Western Front came during the morning of June 19. In twelve short minutes he excelled himelf, as his last combat report shows.

Once or twice the idea that a live man had been piloting the machine would occur and recur to me, and it would worry me a bit. My sleep would be spoiled perhaps for a night. I did not relish the idea even of killing Germans, yet, when in a combat in the air, it seemed more like any other kind of sport, and to shoot down a machine was very much the same as if one were shooting down clay pigeons. One had the great satisfaction of feeling that one had hit the target and brought it down; that one was victorious again.

Combats in the Air

Squadron: No. 85
Type and No. of Aeroplane: S.E.5a C1904
Armament: 1 Lewis and 1 Vickers
Pilot: Major W. A. Bishop V.C., D.S.O., M.C.
Observer:
Destroyed: 5
Driven down out of control:
Driven down:

Date: 19th June 1918
Time:
Locality:

Height:

1,100 feet. 1 mile east of Ploegsteert. 9.58 a.m.

After crossing the lines in the clouds I came out over Ploegsteert Wood, saw three Pfalz scouts which I attacked. Two other Pfalz then approached from east. I fired short burst into one of original three enemy aircraft. He went down in a vertical dive. Second and third enemy aircraft then while circling about me collided and fell together. First enemy aircraft crashed and burst into flames 1 1/2 miles east of Ploegsteert. Remaining two enemy aircraft turned and flew east. I gave chase and opened fire on one at 200 yards range, enemy aircraft spun into ground. Last enemy aircraft zoomed into clouds and escaped.

900 feet. Between Neuve Eglise and Ploegsteert at 10.10 a.m.

I met a two-seater and attacked from behind and underneath. Enemy aircraft burst into flames. I then fired on a small body of troops on the ground scattering them. Climbed into clouds and flew west.

(Sgd) W. A. Bishop Major Commanding 85 Squadron.

Very few pilots achieved five victories in one day, let alone within a twelve minute period! But it was time to leave No. 85 Sqdn, albeit briefly, to the capable leadership of Mick Mannock. There were administrative duties concerning the formation of a Canadian Air Force and Bishop had already written to Brig.-Gen. E. W. B. Morrison, the officer in charge of artillery in the Canadian Expeditionary Force. Responding to complaints from Morrison that too many men were being transferred to the Royal Air Force and depleting his batteries, Bishop expressed his own view that Canadians should constitute a separate air arm:

66 Under the present circumstances, Canadians in the RAF, although doing remarkably well, are certainly not doing as well as if they were in a Canadian Corps for the reasons that (1) They are in a great many circumstances working under senior officers who do not understand them. (2) ...nor often appreciate their different point of view. (3) They have not the personal touch with their country which branches of the Canadian Corps have and consequently are not inspired by direct connection with the country they are fighting for and the people at home. 99

Bishop believed that Canadian airmen should work with Canadian Army units to improve morale and give the men some affiliation rather than have them operate with, and supposedly

Left
The war was over for Bishop when he returned from his last patrol having shot down five enemy aircraft, a remarkable feat by any standard, and one which officially carried him into second position behind Mick Mannock in the list of Allied aces.

for, the British. Clearly, the British perception of where Canada stood in relation to the Mother Country was different to the Canadian view and the reasons they were fighting at all were derived from a wholly different perspective. Bishop was transferred to Canadian H.Q. in London on August 5 and became embroiled in a bitter internal debate within the top ranks of Canadian political opinion about the formation of a Canadian Air Force and a Royal Canadian Naval Air Service. He was given leave to return to Canada and present a case for amalgamating the two proposed services; neither had yet been formed. He was given the temporary rank of Lieutenant Colonel and placed in charge of selecting officers and men for two new squadrons staffed entirely by Canadians. One was to have been a fighter squadron equipped with Sopwith Dolphins and the other a bomber squadron with D.H.9s. Bishop wanted Major Raymond Collishaw to command the fighter squadron and selected Captain Walter B. Lawson for command of the bomber squadron. Major Collishaw was not available, so Bishop put Captain A. E. McKeever in his place.

There was a rich pool of Canadian pilots from which to select.

66 A new kind of enemy was meeting us now - a two-seater machine which mounted a small cannon, or shell-firing gun. This was a sort of 'pom-pom' gun, discharging about a one-pound shell, which would either burst upon percussion or after travelling a certain distance through the air. Several times, while attacking machines doing artillery work, we were surprised to see little white puffs around us, and realised suddenly that these were small bursting shells. 99

Of the top eight British aces, one came from South Africa, one came from Australia and four from Canada: Billy Bishop, Raymond Collishaw, Donald MacLaren and William Barker. Of the other two, one was an Irishman, the other an Englishman. Born in British Columbia, Collishaw served with the Royal Naval Air Service from 1916 and scored 60 victories. Donald MacLaren originated in Ottawa, joined the RFC in November 1917 and rose to command of No. 46 Sqdn, eventually scoring 54 victories. William Barker came from Manitoba and transferred from his regiment to the RFC late in 1915, scoring 53 victories.

Not one of the Canadians was defeated in combat and two received the Victoria Cross. Nominated for No. 1 Squadron in

66 All fights vary slightly in the tactics required, and it is necessary to think quickly and act instantly. Where a large number of machines are engaged, one great thing is always to be the upper man - that is, to be slightly higher than your particular opponent. With this extra height it is quite easy to dive upon him, and it makes manoeuvring much easier. If, as is often the case, you are the 'under dog', it is a very difficult position, and requires great care to carry on the fight with any chance of success. Every time your opponent attempts to dive at you or attack you in any way, the best thing to do is to turn on him, pull the nose of your machine up, and fire. 99

Right
No. 85 Sqdn, RFC, was a brief and not altogether successful assignment for the lone fighter, Canada's leading ace choosing to engage the enemy unaccompanied by other members of his squadron.

the anticipated Canadian Air Force, Andrew McKeever was born in Ontario and arrived with the Canadian Expeditionary Force at the outbreak of war. He transferred to the RFC in December 1916, scored thirty victories in six months and spent the last ten months of the war as a flying instructor in England. He too survived until an automobile accident in 1919 inflicted injuries from which he died on Christms Day.

In the official list of victory logs, the top seven British aces destroyed a total 423 aircraft, of which 239 (56%) were credited to the four Canadians. Bishop had been given responsibility for liaison with the RAF and for setting up the organisation and training programme for the new CAF. But it was not to be. Bishop relinquished this position in early October and sailed for Canada, leaving unfinished business which slowed the formation of the CAF. On his way back to his home country Bishop received news that an armistice had been signed and the fighting was over.

Bishop was demobilised on the last days of 1918. He had written a book and it was selling well. However, Bishop wanted to keep his hand in at flying his beloved aircraft, and teamed with William Barker to form Bishop-Barker Aeroplanes Ltd of Toronto. The company acquired forty Curtiss JN4 trainers put back into the hands of the Imperial Munitions Board as obsolescent aircraft, but did not survive long. Bishop smashed up a Sopwith Dove two-seater in 1920 which had been used by Barker to fly the Prince of Wales around Hounslow, England, in May 1919. Receiving severe facial injuries, Bishop got a broken nose and double vision which finally prevented him flying.

A year later the company was dissolved. Barker eventually joined the Canadian Air Force and was killed in an air accident in 1930. Billy and Margaret Bishop had a difficult time when their first child died three weeks after birth. They came to England to put the tragedy behind them and to build Billy's business interests, settling into a fashionable house in Chester Terrace alongside Regents Park. The couple had many friends in England from the days when Billy was a hero, eagerly sought by socialites to show off to friends and relatives. They quickly found their feet, numbering Winston Churchill among their friends and building a reputable business.

When the depression hit in 1929, the Bishops had two young children and a high life which soon disappeared when they lost their total investments in stocks and shares. Once again a friend was there when needed and Billy was appointed vice-president of the McColl-Frontenac Oil Company of Canada. In 1931, Bishop was made an honorary Group Captain in the Royal Canadian Air Force and persistently lobbied for better air defence, pointing out the threat posed by German rearmament. In 1936 his efforts were further rewarded when he was promoted to honorary Air Vice-Marshal and given the task of generating popular support for the RCAF.

As war clouds once again gathered in Europe, Bishop became an Air Marshal and was put in charge of the Air Advisory Committee. Then, when war finally came in 1939 he was made Director of Recruiting. Throwing himself wholeheartedly into

“The idea of killing was, of course, always against my nature, but for two reasons I did not mind it: one, and the greater one, of course, being that it was another Hun down, and so much more good done in the war; secondly, it was paying back some of the debts I owed the Huns for robbing me of the best friends possible. Then, too, in the air one did not altogether feel the human side of it. As I have said before, it was not like killing a man so much as just bringing down a bird in sport.”

" In going into a fight now, I felt none of those thrills which I used to feel at first. I was quite cool and collected, but probably did not enjoy it as much as I did in the days when a certain amount of anxiety and fear was felt just before the fight started. But the moment my machine gun commenced to fire, I felt the old feeling of exultation, and this always remained with me throughout the whole of every fight I have had."

the effort at the expense of his health, he was made a CB in the King's Birthday Honours List during June 1944. Still he worked on, far beyond the expectations placed upon his office, wearing himself down in the process.

After the war, Billy Bishop returned to Montreal and the oil business before taking early retirement in 1952. His strength sapped, he was in poor health and suffered several illnesses. Each winter was spent in Florida, where a servant took care of both Billy and Margaret. In 1956 Billy felt too tired and exhausted to make the long trip back to Canada but Margaret went to see her son in Edmonton before the winter set in. On the evening of September 10, Billy told their servant, Lethbridge, that he felt better than he had for a long time and retired to bed. One hour after midnight, he died peacefully in his sleep, on September 11, 1956.

Somewhere across the cloud filled skies that cover a place once called the Western Front the echo from a rare sound can be heard drifting over the millions of crosses that line the cemetery at Verdun, where so many Canadians were lost, or the unknown dead at Ypres. It is the sound of a sputtering rotary engine and the occasional brief burst from a Lewis gun as a laughing young Canadian charges toward the gathering dusk. For Billy Bishop's spirit lives on and will always be seen fleetingly, dashing across the sky in its silver aeroplane, by those still alive who pause and quietly remember the dark days of the first war in the air and a very brave airman who will always live on in their affections.

CHAPTER SIX *Technical Details*

Technical details of the
fighting machines flown by
William Avery Bishop and a full
log of all his victories.

*"I am of the opinion that the R.E.7 with
120 hp Beardmore engine is useless in the
field. The lifting power of the machine
rapidly decreases, and although the
engines appear to be running now better
than they ever did . . . not half of the
machines can get off the ground if it is at
all sticky with full load, nor can they
climb to 8,000 ft. "*

HUGH TRENCHARD, MARCH 8, 1916

**From The Aeroplanes of the Royal Flying Corps (Military
Wing) by J. M. Bruce, courtesy Conway Maritime Press.**

Victory Log of William Avery (Billy) Bishop, V.C., D.S.O. and Bar, M.C., D.F.C., C.C.L.d'H., C. de G.

Victory logs of World War I air aces are notoriously suspect, not because of any deliberate attempt to make false claims, but because the necessary corroboration was frequently waived. It is also important to remember that much detail of individual combats can now only come from existing records. We are fast approaching the time when no aviator from World War I remains alive and there are disputes and enigmas that will for ever remain unsolved.

In the case of Billy Bishop, a great deal remains to be understood about the majority of his combats. Only a few of his many fights were witnessed or confirmed by a third party. Such is the lot of the lone aviator who chooses to seek out the enemy alone and without assistance. Bishop was remarkably successful, although some combat locations remain unknown. For instance, the airfield he attacked during the morning of

DATE	TIME	A/c FLOWN	A/c CLAIMED	LOCATION
1917 Mar 25	17:00	Nieuport A306	Albatros D.III	North of St. Leger
1917 Mar 31	07:30	Nieuport A6769	Albatros D.III	South of Gavrelle
1917 Apr 6	09:35	Nieuport A6769	Albatros D.III	Cherisy
1917 Apr 7	17:00	Nieuport A6769	Albatros D.III	Arras
1917 Apr 7	17:10	Nieuport A6769	Kite Balloon	Vis-en-Artois
1917 Apr 8	09:30	Nieuport A6769	Albatros C.V	Douai-Fouquieres
1917 Apr 8	09:30	Nieuport A6769	Albatros D.V	North-east Arras
1917 Apr 8	09:40	Nieuport A6769	Kite Balloon	Arras
1917 Apr 8	09:45	Nieuport A6769	A.E.G. C.IV?	East of Arras
1917 Apr 8	10:10	Nieuport A6769	Albatros D.III	Vitry
1917 Apr 20	14:58	Nieuport B1566	Aviatik C	Biache-St. Vaast
1917 Apr 22	11:20	Nieuport B1566	Albatros D.III	Vis-en-Artois
1917 Apr 22	11:21	Nieuport B1566	Albatros D.III	Vis-en-Artois
1917 Apr 23	15:46	Nieuport B1566	Albatros C.III	Vitry
1917 Apr 23	15:59	Nieuport B1566	Albatros D.III	East of Vitry
1917 Apr 27	08:55	Nieuport B1566	Kite Balloon	Vitry
1917 Apr 29	11:55	Nieuport B1566	Halb' D.III	East of Epinoy
1917 Apr 30	11:15	Nieuport B1566	Av'/Alb C.III?	South-east of Lens
1917 Apr 30	11:15	Nieuport B1566	Albatros C	Wancourt-S Lens
1917 Apr 30	12:08	Nieuport B1566	Albatros C.III	Monchy-S Lens
1917 May 2	10:10	Nieuport B1566	Albatros C.III	East of Epinoy
1917 May 2	10:12	Nieuport B1566	Albatros C.III	East of Epinoy
1917 May 2	12:20	Nieuport B1566	Albatros	East of Lens
1917 May 4	13:30	Nieuport B1566	A.E.G. C.V	Brebieres-Vitry
1917 May 7	09:50	Nieuport B1566	Albatros D.III	North of Vitry
1917 May 7	15:00	Nieuport B1566	Albatros D.III	Brebieres
1917 May 26	10:16	Nieuport B1566	Albatros D.?	Izel-les-Epeurchin
1917 May 27	09:40	Nieuport B1566	Rump'/Av' C.?	Dourges-Monchy
1917 May 31	19:11	Nieuport B1566	Albatros D.V?	Epinoy
1917 Jun 2	04:23	Nieuport B1566	Albatros D.III	?
1917 Jun 2	?	Nieuport B1566	Albatros D.III	?

June 2, 1917, has never been found and its location has remained a mystery despite concerted efforts to find it.

In the table that follows a record is given of every combat for which there is very strong circumstantial evidence that, accepting Bishop's description of the encounter, he should be rightfully credited with the destruction of an aircraft, a balloon or a victory shared with another pilot. The 'official' score is also recorded but the reader might like to ponder whether two aircraft that collided on June 19, 1918, while Bishop was in the vicinity can be legitimately included in his victory log. Also, the two shared victories are counted as single scores.

Nevertheless, the reader will note that Bishop has submitted reports that indicate his true score may have been closer to 80 than the 72 for which most sources give him credit. As is the intent of this Famous Flyers series, the reader is left to judge from the facts presented.

66 Along with the new ambition there was born in me as well a distinct dislike for all two-seated German flying machines! They always seemed so placid and sort of contented with themselves. I picked a fight with the two-seaters wherever I could find one, and I searched for them high and low. Many people think of the two-seater as a superior fighting machine because of its greater gun-power. But to me they always seemed fair prey and an easy target.99

SCORE A	B	REMARKS AND COMMENTS
1	1	Aircraft confirmed out of control by anti-aircraft guns
2	2	Aircraft confirmed out of control by anti-aircraft guns
3		Not officially attributed. Pilot probably Eicholz, killed
4	3	Driven down out of control. Inconclusive combat
5		Not officially attributed. Balloon seen going down in smoke
6		Shared with Maj. Scott and observed to crash. Observer hit
7	4	Driven down out of control
8		Balloon attacked at 5,000 ft but did not smoke on descent
9	5	Some doubt exists over the type of aircraft driven down
10	6	Maj. Scott wanted Bishop credited 6 kills this day
11	7	Went down in flames
12	8	Victory achieved while flying with his patrol
13	9	Aircraft observed to break away under control and descend
14	10	Aircraft forced to land and crew wounded in action
15	11	Aircraft destroyed
16		Balloon was totally destroyed in the attack
17	12	Aircraft went down in flames and was destroyed
18	13	One of two engaged. A/c believed to have crashed
19		The second of two engaged. Believed forced down and landed
20	14	Last of eight a/c involved in Bishop's combats within 2 hrs
21	15	First of two victories obtained after leaving patrol
22	16	Driven down out of control
23	17	A/c driven down and may have been forced to land
24		Shared with Lt. Fry and seen to crash
25	18	A/c driven down and observed to be smoking
26	19	Driven down out of control
27	20	Driven down out of control but not seen to crash
28	21	Believed to have crashed
29	22	A/c believed to have crashed but not observed
30	23	First of 3 a/c destroyed in airfield raid, location unknown
31	24	Airfield location believed Estourniel, Esnes or Awoignt

DATE	TIME	A/c FLOWN	A/c CLAIMED	LOCATION
1917 Jun 2	05:00	Nieuport B1566	Albatros D.III	?
1917 Jun 8	12:10	Nieuport B1566	Albatros D.III	North of Lille
1917 Jun 24	11:23	Nieuport B1566	Albatros D.III	Beaumont
1917 Jun 25	10:25	Nieuport B1566	Albatros D.III	Dury
1917 Jun 26	10:55	Nieuport B1566	Albatros D.III	Annay/N. of Etaing
1917 Jun 26	10:55	Nieuport B1566	Albatros D.III	Annay/N. of Etaing
1917 Jun 28	11:30	Nieuport B1566	Albatros D.III	Drocourt/La Bassee
1917 Jul 10	20:10	Nieuport B1566	Albatros D.III	Vitry-Quiery
1917 Jul 12	13:30	Nieuport B1566	Albatros D.III	Vitry-Douai
1917 Jul 17	19:43	Nieuport B1566	Albatros D.III	Havrincourt
1917 Jul 17	19:55	Nieuport B1566	Albatros D.III	Marquion-Queant
1917 Jul 20	12:05	Niueport B1566	Albatros D.III	S.E. Havrincourt
1917 Jul 28	18:10	S.E.5 A8936	Albatros D.III	Phalempin
1917 Jul 29	07:10	S.E.5 A8936	Albatros D.III	Beaumont
1917 Aug 5	20:00	S.E.5 A8936	Albatros D.III	Hendecourt-Monchy
1917 Aug 5	20:20	S.E.5 A8930	Albatros D.III	Hendecourt-Monchy
1917 Aug 6	15:45	S.E.5 A8936	Albatros D.V	Brebieres
1917 Aug 9	09:00	S.E.5 A8936	Albatros C.V	Ecourt-St. Quentin
1917 Aug 13	19:02	S.E.5 A8936	Albatros D.III	South of Douai
1917 Aug 13	19:05	S.E.5 A8936	Albatros D.III	South of Douai
1917 Aug 15	20:20	S.E.5 A8936	Albatros C.?	Henin-Lietard
1917 Aug 16	19:03	S.E.5 A8936	Aviatik C.?	Harnes
1917 Aug 16	19:06	S.E.5 A8936	Albatros D.III	Carvin
1918 May 27	16:32	S.E.5a C6490	Av'/Alb' C.?	Houthulst Forest
1918 May 28	15:00	S.E.5a C6490	Pfalz D.III	North of Ypres
1918 May 30	15:42	S.E.5a C6490	Av'/Alb' C.?	Roulers
1918 May 30	15:45	S.E.5a C6490	Av'/Alb' C.?	Roulers
1918 May 30	17:53	S.E.5 C6490	Albatros D.V	Armentieres
1918 May 31	15:05	S.E.5a C6490	Pfalz D.III	Armentieres
1918 May 31	15:15	S.E.5a C6490	Av'/Alb.C?	South-west Lille
1918 May 31	20:15	S.E.5a C6490	Pfalz D.III	North of Estaires
1918 Jun 1	20:10	S.E.5a C6490	Pfalz D.III	La Gorgue
1918 Jun 2	20:10	S.E.5a C6490	Pfalz D.III	Armentieres
1918 Jun 4	11:28	S.E.5a C6490	Albatros D.?	Nieuport-Ostend
1918 Jun 4	11:37	S.E.5a C6490	Albatros D.?	Leaffinghe
1918 Jun 15	18:55	S.E.5a C1904	Pfalz D.III	East of Estaires
1918 Jun 16	20:20	S.E.5a C1904	Av'/Alb.C?	Armentieres
1918 Jun 16	20:28	S.E.5a C1904	Albatros D.?	Armentieres
1918 Jun 17	10:25	S.E.5a C1904	Av'/Alb.C?	Staden
1918 Jun 17	10:50	S.E.5a C1904	Albatros D.?	Sailley-sur-Lys
1918 Jun 17	10:55	S.E.5a C1904	Av/Alb.C?	Nr Laventie
1918 Jun 18	10:45	S.E.5a C1904	Albatros D.?	6 mls NE of Ypres
1918 Jun 18	10:45	S.E.5a C1904	Albatros D.?	6 mls NE of Ypres
1918 Jun 19	09:58	S.E.5a C1904	Pfalz D.III	E. of Ploegsteert
1918 Jun 19	09:58	S.E.5a C1904	Pfalz D.III	E. of Ploegsteert
1918 Jun 19	09:58	S.E.5a C1904	Pfalz D.III	E. of Ploegsteert
1918 Jun 19	09:58	S.E.5a C1904	Pfalz D.III	E. of Ploegsteert
1918 Jun 19	10:10	S.E.5a C1904	L.V.G. C.?	Neuve Eglise/Plo'

SCORE A	B	REMARKS AND COMMENTS
32	25	No positive identification of airfield established
33	26	A/c one of 4 engaged within 37 min period beginning 11:40
34	27	A/c destroyed in flames during a lone patrol unwitnessed
35	28	Inconclusive. One of group engaged by 3 pilots with Bishop
36	29	Seen to go down in flames while attacking two a/c
37	30	Went down apparently out of control
38	31	A/c broke up; wings came off. One of 4 enemy a/c on patrol
39	32	A/c driven down out of control during accompanied patrol
40	33	One of 6 a/c engaged by patrol, only 3 escaped
41	34	One of two attacked at 13,000 ft; went down in flames
42	35	Tailplane broke off enemy a/c and it fell out of control
43	36	One of a pair attacked at 13,500 ft with only 15 rounds
44	37	First victory with new S.E.5. A/c destroyed in flames
45	38	The patrol attacked 4 enemy a/c. Rest escaped
46	39	One of 8 a/c engaged; went down in flames; 6 escaped
47	40	Second of 8 engaged this patrol; went down out of control
48	41	Identified in combat report as a D.IV. Impossible; 1 built
49	42	Sustained attack from 14,000 ft down to 6,000 ft
50	43	A/c burst into flames at 11,000 ft
51	44	A/c burst into flames. Bishop attacked another; it escaped
52	45	Fired 30 rounds from 100 yds on rearmost a/c of 3
53	46	Attacked at 14,000 ft. Both wings came off in halves
54	47	Fired 80 rounds at 13,000 ft altitude. Seen to crash
55	48	Stalked a/c for long time. Wings broke off
56	49	Attacked at 12,000 ft after stalking at 15,000 ft
57	50	One of two two-seaters attacked
58	51	Unidentified two-seater paired with previous victory
59	52	Attacked and destroyed at 15,400 ft
60	53	A/c attacked at 14,000 ft 5 mls north of Armentieres
61	54	A/c dived towards the left and descended to land in field
62	55	Fired 20 rounds at 50 yds range. A/c broke up in flight
63	56	With 4 on patrol, attacked 6 a/c; 4 shot down, 2 escaped
64	57	Victory secured while flying alone and unescorted
65	58	Attacked at 14,000 ft 3 mls out to sea. A/c crashed to sea
66	59	Attacked silver a/c from 15,000 ft. Fell out of control
67	60	One of 4 attacked at 17,500 ft, with black wings/red fuse
68	61	A/c destroyed and seen to burst into flames
69	62	A/c one of 4 attacking Bishop at 8,000 ft. Seen to crash
70	63	A/c approaching British lines. Burst into flames
71	64	Seen to crash after expending 15 rounds
72	65	Attacked twice and a/c seen to crash on road near Laventie
73	66	One of 4 enemy a/c attacked. Apparently exploded in flames
74	67	Seen to smoke and then burst into flames; 2 others fled
75	68	One of 3 Pfalz scouts attacked at 1,100 ft
76	69	One of two a/c which collided during fight with Bishop
77	70	Second of two a/c which collided during fight with Bishop
78	71	Fired upon from 200 yds and a/c seen to spin into ground
79	72	Attacked from behind and below and seen to erupt in flames

R.E.7

Billy Bishop was to spend much of the early part of his flying career on the second seat of the R.E.7, a two-seat reconnaissance bomber which first appeared in spring 1915. It derived from the R.E.5, latest in a short line of Reconnaissance Experimental aircraft first produced in 1912. It epitomised the classic interpretation of aircraft in war defined by the British Army: a stable aircraft from which an observer could scan the ground below and write his intelligence report before flying home to deliver it. In short, a variation of the role performed by the gas filled balloon used since the American Civil War for spying on the enemy and directing artillery fire.

Free to roam the skies at will, an aeroplane would be so much better than a tethered balloon. When in 1912 the Royal Aircraft Factory, Farnborough, England, set about the task of designing a Reconnaissance Experimental aircraft it incorporated lessons from work by Edward Teshmaker Busk on aircraft stability and control. When the R.E.1 appeared in July 1913, it was the first inherently stable aeroplane designed at Farnborough and first in a long line of R.E. types that would see service throughout World War I.

Only two R.E.1s were ever built and the second was sent to France, serving briefly with No. 2 Sqdn, RFC. The type had a maximum speed of 78 mph and a stalling speed of 48 mph with a climb rate of 600 ft/min. Designed and produced in 1913 as a Hydro Reconnaissance Experimental aircraft, the one H.R.E.2 that followed the R.E.1 could fly on and off water using floats instead of wheels, although a conventional landing gear was optional. The R.E.3 was the H.R.E.2 with a 120 hp Austro-Daimler engine while the R.E.4 was a rotary engined two-seater designed but never built.

The R.E.5 appeared in late 1913 and 25 were ordered by the then Secretary of State for War, Colonel J. E. B. Seely, using money obtained from the Navy in exchange for the Army's airships; the government had decided that the Navy should take responsibility for the nation's lighter-than-air devices owned by the armed services and gave the Army £25,000 for them. The R.E.5 was a larger and heavier version of the R.E.1 and power was provided by a 120 hp Austro-Daimler engine protected by a hooded cowling encasing a radiator to the rear. It had a span of 45 ft 4 in and the fuselage was deep, providing two cockpits, one for the pilot and a forward cockpit for the observer.

The aircraft carried a single 0.303 in Lewis gun and various small arms with provision for 20 lb Hales bombs. Unusually for the period, the aircraft incorporated steel tubing in the fuselage and a twin skid forward of the main wheels. The R.E.5 was delivered for flying tests in late January 1914. About fifteen R.E.5s had been completed when war broke out on August 4, 1914. Some problems had been experienced with the engines and the crankshafts had to be replaced.

A variant had emerged with long span upper wings, extended to 57 ft 3 in, and one of these had been flown to the then record altitude of 18,900 ft. Intended as long range aircraft and with extra tanks for additional fuel, it was one of several aircraft of this type used for a variety of experimental tasks. One at least was fitted for early radio trials. Some had experimental air brakes and this modification was one of several that carried forward to the R.E.7.

No. 6 Squadron, RFC, was the first unit to receive the R.E.5 although the squadron was dispersed to provide equipment for Nos. 2, 3, 4 and 5 Sqdns, RFC, that went to France when war broke out. The greatest user of the R.E.5 was No. 7 Squadron which did good work in the early months using the aircraft for reconnaissance and early bombing activities, although the load was limited and it would not have survived had it been called upon to defend itself against single-seat fighters when they appeared in late 1915.

But neither was the R.E.7 much good at that and it was asked to soldier on long after it should have been replaced. The R.E.7

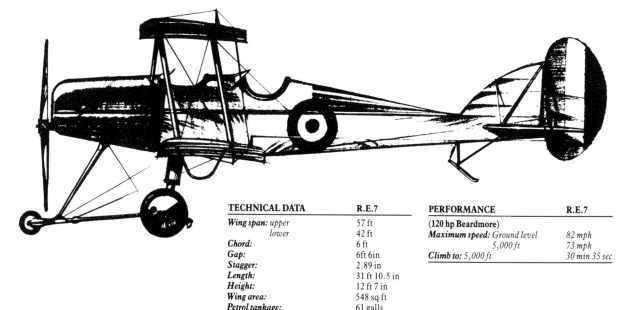

TECHNICAL DATA	R.E.7
Wing span: upper	57 ft
lower	42 ft
Chord:	6 ft
Gap:	6ft 6in
Stagger:	2.89 in
Length:	31 ft 10.5 in
Height:	12 ft 7 in
Wing area:	548 sq ft
Petrol tankage:	61 galls
Weight: empty	2,285 lb
loaded:	3,290 lb

PERFORMANCE	R.E.7
(120 hp Beardmore)	
Maximum speed: Ground level	82 mph
5,000 ft	73 mph
Climb to: 5,000 ft	30 min 35 sec

appeared as a robust and beefed up version of the R.E.5 but with many improvements. It had oleo legs, telescoping cylinders filled with oil that absorbed the impact of landing, and air brakes - a novel feature for 1915! The R.E.7 was sent to No. 12 Squadron in France during September 1915, but deliveries were slow; only sixteen had arrived by the end of the year.

The R.E.7 had the extended wing of the derivative R.E.5, and a fuselage carrying the same two-seat arrangement although later versions had a variety of optional positions for the defensive Lewis gun. Unfortunately, it also had the 120 hp Beardmore engine, encased within a cowling similar to that attached to its

predecessor. The R.E.7 was built to carry a single 336 lb bomb but that was a farcical expectation. Grossly underpowered, the aircraft was inadequate for the assigned task and several were used as escorts for other aircraft employed as bombers.

No. 21 Squadron in which Billy Bishop served for five months in 1916 arrived in France during late January that year. Their R.E.7s were clearly incapable of carrying out the mission of reconnaissance and bombing although the type struggled on throughout the year until replaced in that squadron by single-seat B.E.12s during August 1916. Paradoxically, two R.E.7s were fitted out as

three-seaters although there is little indication as to precisely what they were intended to do, or achieved.

The R.E.7 was tried out with several different engines including the 190 hp Rolls Royce Falcon, the 200 hp RAF3a, the 220 hp Renault, the 225 hp Sunbeam and the 250 hp Rolls Royce Eagle. Powered by the 150 hp twelve-cylinder air-cooled RAF4a engine, their greatest glory came during June and July 1916 when several R.E.7s from No. 21 Squadron carried out offensive bombing raids. It was their last, albeit credible, appearance and by the end of 1916 the R.E.7 had more or less passed into history.

NIEUPORT TYPE 17

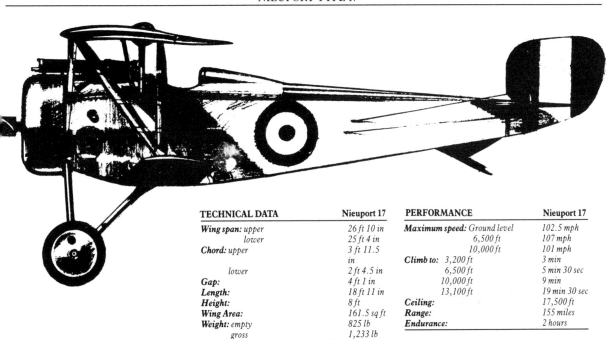

TECHNICAL DATA	Nieuport 17
Wing span: upper	26 ft 10 in
lower	25 ft 4 in
Chord: upper	3 ft 11.5 in
lower	2 ft 4.5 in
Gap:	4 ft 1 in
Length:	18 ft 11 in
Height:	8 ft
Wing Area:	161.5 sq ft
Weight: empty	825 lb
gross	1,233 lb

PERFORMANCE	Nieuport 17
Maximum speed: Ground level	102.5 mph
6,500 ft	107 mph
10,000 ft	101 mph
Climb to: 3,200 ft	3 min
6,500 ft	5 min 30 sec
10,000 ft	9 min
13,100 ft	19 min 30 sec
Ceiling:	17,500 ft
Range:	155 miles
Endurance:	2 hours

Billy Bishop scored 36 of his 72 official victories in a Nieuport 17 yet he flew this type for only four months. Because the fame he rapidly achieved was built during the period he had use of a Nieuport 17, he is forever associated with it, although half his score was logged on an S.E.5 or S.E.5a. The Societe Anonyme des Etablissements Nieport had been set up by the French designer Edouard de Nieport in 1909 and went on to produce a successful series of monoplanes over the next five years. Edouard was killed in 1911 and his brother took over the firm until he too was killed in 1913.

Early in 1914 the company employed Gustave Delage to design a small biplane for the Gordon Bennett Trophy air race, which was to have been held during September at the small airfield of Buc on the outskirts of Paris. When France went to war with Germany at the beginning of August the race was cancelled but a tiny biplane had appeared specially for the race which was to influence a long line of Nieuport fighters during World War I.

Because the Gordon Bennett Trophy race required participating aircraft to have a particularly low minimum flying speed,

Delage designed a biplane called the Nieuport 10 with a narrow-chord bottom wing which could be made to rotate around the single spar. This variable incidence was made possible by vee-shaped interplane struts converging at the bottom wing on a hinged pivot. To use the lower wing as an air brake the pilot could vary the incidence and dramatically cut the speed of the aircraft. The pitch of the bottom wing would be returned by the pilot to normal incidence, thus providing control over a wide range of speeds and flying conditions.

Initially designed as a single-seater it was adapted for military service, with a fixed bottom wing, as a two-seater in two versions. One, with an observer and his gun in front of the pilot, known as the 10 AV, and another with the observer behind the pilot known as the 10 AR. Powered by an 80 hp Le Rhone or Anzani rotary engine, the Type 10 had a top speed of only 87 mph and took 16 minutes to reach 6,500 ft. It was frequently flown as a single-seater. A larger and more powerful derivative known as the Type 12 appeared in 1915.

Meanwhile, exploiting the virtues of the sesquiplane configuration, retained by M. Delage to avoid the argument then raging over whether a monoplane or a biplane was best, the single seat Type 11 appeared in 1915. This was the original design concept developed for the Gordon Bennett Trophy and defined the shape and appearance of the single-seat Nieuport scout as it evolved through Types 16, 17, 21, 23, 24 and 27. The diminutive Type 11 had a wing span of 24.6 ft, a length of 18.5 ft and a height of 8.8 ft.

Wing area was increased by 15.4% but the sesquiplane configuration was retained, both top and bottom wings being increased in size proportionally. This helped improve the poor handling characteristics of the Type 11 over the Type 11. Retaining the box section fuselage aft of the pilot's cockpit, the forward fuselage was fully faired to meet the circular engine cowling which featured two ventilation holes. With reduced gap between the wings the aircraft was lower and the top wing was closer to the fuselage, held in place by two short vertical struts forward and a short inverted vee-strut at the rear just in front of the cockpit. A head rest, first attached to the Nieuport 16, was provided for the pilot.

The Type 17 appeared in mid-1916 and was an immediate success. It was responsible along with the British Airco D.H.2 for defeating the Fokker monoplanes with their synchronised machine guns. Several famous and very successful French pursuit squadrons flew the Type 17. Derivatives included the 17bis equipped with a 130 hp Clerget 9B engine, the Type 21 with an 80 or 120 hp Le Rhone and enlarged ailerons, the Type 23 with its machine gun mounted on the starboard side of the forward fuselage, the Type 24 with a circular cross section fuselage and the Type 27 with the Type 24 fuselage and a small fin forward of the rudder, rounded wing tips and horizontal tail and a 120 hp Le Rhone rotary engine.

These were the last vee-strut Nieuports derived from a tiny sesquiplane first designed for a peaceful air contest in the last year of peace. By the end of summer 1917 the Nieuport vee-strutters were looking, and performing, like tired old veterans. But they still had useful roles to perform. That they lived on through several variants and derivatives to the end of the war, and found use afterwards, is a tribute to the soundness and logic of simplicity in aircraft design.

The aircraft adopted standard wood and fabric construction but differed from the Nieuport 12 in that the top wing had two spars. It also had unequal chord ailerons and the vee-shaped interplane struts were bound with tape and wire braced. Four vertical centre-section struts held the top wing above the forward fuselage. The lower wing had slight dihedral, giving the sesquiplane its characteristic look in the air. The top wing had exactly twice the wing area of the bottom wing.

The wooden box fuselage had a rounded top decking with pronounced upward sweep behind the engine and modest vertical taper toward the tail. The tailplane was fabric covered steel tubing. The vertical rudder and horizontal tail had raked tips. The 80 hp Gnome rotary engine was faired to the box section fuselage with small triangular metal fairings. Conventional vee-shaped undercarriage struts and leaf type spring tail skid were attached to the lower fuselage. Because of its size, the aircraft was dubbed 'Bebe' and appeared in French and Belgian units from summer 1915.

Simplicity being the cornerstone of its design, the Type 11 was fitted with a Lewis gun over the top of the upper wing to fire forward outside the propeller arc. By early 1916, it had been fitted with the more powerful 110 hp Le Rhone 9J engine and designated Type 16. This version served with the Royal Flying Corps and became the first of all subsequent Nieuport single-seat scouts to carry the Lewis gun on a Foster mounting. Developed by Sgt. R. G. Foster of No. 11 Squadron, RFC, the mounting enabled the pilot to pull the gun back and down from over the top wing and change drums.

With additional power, the Type 16 had a top speed of 103 mph versus 97 mph for the Type 11 and was a popular fighting scout throughout 1916. It was increasingly supplemented, however, by the Type 17. This aircraft was a redesigned Type 11 with the engine of the Type 16. It had a top speed of 107 mph and could reach 6,500 ft in just over five minutes, half the time taken by the Type 11. The Type 17 looked considerably more robust and with a redesigned fuselage was more streamlined.

S.E.5/S.E.5a

Fully one half of Billy Bishop's official victory log lists aircraft driven down while he was flying an S.E.5 or an S.E.5a during July and August 1917 and in May and June 1918. The S.E.5 design had been drawn up in mid-1916 around a 200 hp Hispano-Suiza engine with a Lewis machine gun firing through the hollow propeller shaft. Designed by Marc Birkigt, the engine was built and tested in the Barcelona, Spain, works of Hispano-Suiza during February 1915 and several examples were returned to France and tested during July. Lt.-Col. H. R. M. Brooke-Popham saw the engine and an order was placed.

At the same time, the Royal Aircraft Factory at Farnborough, England, was developing a new

fighter designated the S.E.5, latest in a line of Santos-Dumont Experimental (S.E.) types originated by the S.E.1 designed by Geoffrey de Havilland and F. M. Green in 1911. Aircraft of the S.E., F.E. (Farman Experimental) and B.E. (Bleriot Experimental) types were re-built from crashed aeroplanes of the parent type brought to Farnborough for 'repair'. Because Farnborough had neither money nor remit to develop indigenously new types, these opportunistic assemblages of distorted wood, wire and canvas allowed Farnborough to re-build the aircraft according to new designs.

The S.E.1, in fact, was a re-built Army Bleriot colloquially known as The Mankiller but it looked like a Santos-Dumont design and the

appellation stuck! The S.E.2 was an original Farnborough design for a single-seat Scout Experimental biplane and appeared in 1912 followed by the S.E.4, one of which was built in June 1914; never built, the S.E.3 was to have been a modified S.E.2.

When the prototype S.E.5 appeared in November 1916, it had the 150 hp Hispano-Suiza and no Lewis gun through the propeller shaft, principally because the engine had a direct-drive and could not facilitate the armament. The British air ace Albert Ball flew the prototype on November 22 and declared his dislike for the type; compared to the nimble Nieuport he had been used to flying it was heavy and cumbersome. Other pilots expressed

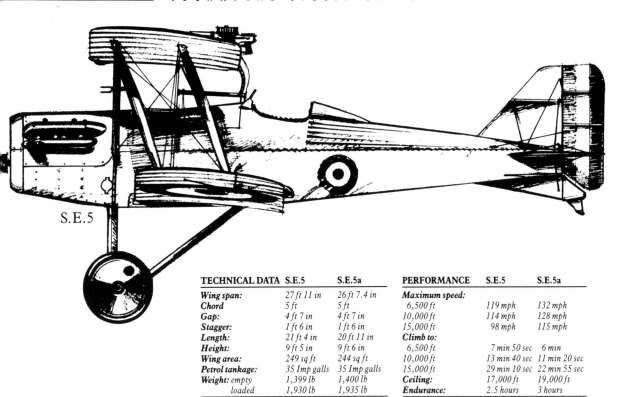

S.E.5

TECHNICAL DATA	S.E.5	S.E.5a		PERFORMANCE	S.E.5	S.E.5a
Wing span:	27 ft 11 in	26 ft 7.4 in		**Maximum speed:**		
Chord	5 ft	5 ft		6,500 ft	119 mph	132 mph
Gap:	4 ft 7 in	4 ft 7 in		10,000 ft	114 mph	128 mph
Stagger:	1 ft 6 in	1 ft 6 in		15,000 ft	98 mph	115 mph
Length:	21 ft 4 in	20 ft 11 in		**Climb to:**		
Height:	9 ft 5 in	9 ft 6 in		6,500 ft	7 min 50 sec	6 min
Wing area:	249 sq ft	244 sq ft		10,000 ft	13 min 40 sec	11 min 20 sec
Petrol tankage:	35 Imp galls	35 Imp galls		15,000 ft	29 min 10 sec	22 min 55 sec
Weight: empty	1,399 lb	1,400 lb		**Ceiling:**	17,000 ft	19,000 ft
loaded	1,930 lb	1,935 lb		**Endurance:**	2.5 hours	3 hours

a liking for the S.E.5, especially when it was taken to France for service trials, in comparison with other Allied scouts designed for a similar role.

The following month it was fitted out to production standard and given a fixed synchronised Vickers gun attached to the port quarter of the forward fuselage and a Lewis gun over the top wing on a Foster mounting. Several modifications had been made. A gravity fuel tank was installed in the top wing centre section replacing the leading edge fuel tank originally designed into the top wing and the wing structure was changed when test pilot Frank Goodden lost his life in the third prototype on January 28, 1917.

This aircraft had the geared 200 hp Hispano-Suiza originally intended for the S.E.5 but production machines had the 150 hp engine. The raked wing tips were more rounded in the production model and the span was reduced. In flight, the S.E.5 proved tough and versatile with a good turn of speed and a brisk performance. It was these qualities that compensated for the lack of agility so favoured by pilots operating the nimble Nieuport sesquiplanes.

No. 56 Squadron was the first Royal Flying

Corps unit to be equipped with the S.E.5. Commanded by Albert Ball who still disliked the type, the squadron would achieve great success with this aircraft. Additional modifications were introduced as early operational flights pointed the way to improvements. No. 56 got its first machines in March 1917, and Ball took his men on their first offensive patrol on April 22. Just four days later he got a double victory and Ball's view of the aircraft changed for the better.

The modifications and changes to the basic design coincided with a switch to the geared 200 hp Hispano-Suiza engine and these collectively introduced the designation S.E.5a, although the engine type has come to popularly differentiate the S.E.5 from the S.E.5a. The first S.E.5a to go to France joined No. 56 Squadron in June 1917. Thereafter all aircraft were produced to the S.E.5a standard but problems with the 200 hp Hispano-Suiza slowed supply to France; only six squadrons had been equipped with them by the end of 1917.

Also, a series of structural failures to the wings caused crashes that brought further modifications to the main spar and the ribs. Several engine manufacturers including Wolseley in England and Brasier in France

produced versions of the 200 hp Hispano-Suiza and each had their special problems. There was an increasing backlog of airframes, built by Martinsyde and Vickers, without engines.

In expectation of better success with the 200 hp Sunbeam Arab, 400 airframes were awaiting engines in January 1918. The Arab proved disappointing and throughout 1918 S.E.5a s gradually adopted the 200 hp Wolseley Viper which was a much modified Hispano-Suiza engine. Although exploited by such well known fighter aces as Mannock, McCudden and Ball, as well as Billy Bishop, the S.E.5a was used in a wide variety of roles.

By the end of the war in November 1918, S.E.5a s had dropped more than 2,200 bombs on ground targets and expended more than 92,000 rounds of ammunition on strafing missions. No less a Royal Flying Corps squadron than the famous No. 56 was withdrawn from France in June 1917 to serve on Home Defence duties playing a part in protecting England from German raiders. In all, 5,205 S.E.5s and S.E.5a s were built. After the war, along with the German Fokker D.VII, several examples were used for barnstorming and film work.

Although America joined the war only 19 months before the Armistice their need for aircraft was large. Without a domestic aircraft design industry capable of supplying indigenous combat planes the United States ordered large numbers from the Allies. The Curtiss Company signed an agreement for the manufacture of 1,000 S.E.5a s but only one all-American S.E.5a had been built when the order was cancelled when the Armistice was signed. A batch of 56 were put together from components shipped from England and 38 had been purchased from the British by the American Expeditionary Force. The Curtiss built S.E.5a were to have been powered by a 180 hp Wright-Martin Hispano-Suiza engine and a 180 hp Wright-Hispano E engine was fitted to 50 S.E.5E aircraft with plywood fuselages put together from spares by a company named Eberhardt. Some British S.E.5a s went to Australia and Canada and one was taken to Japan in 1921.

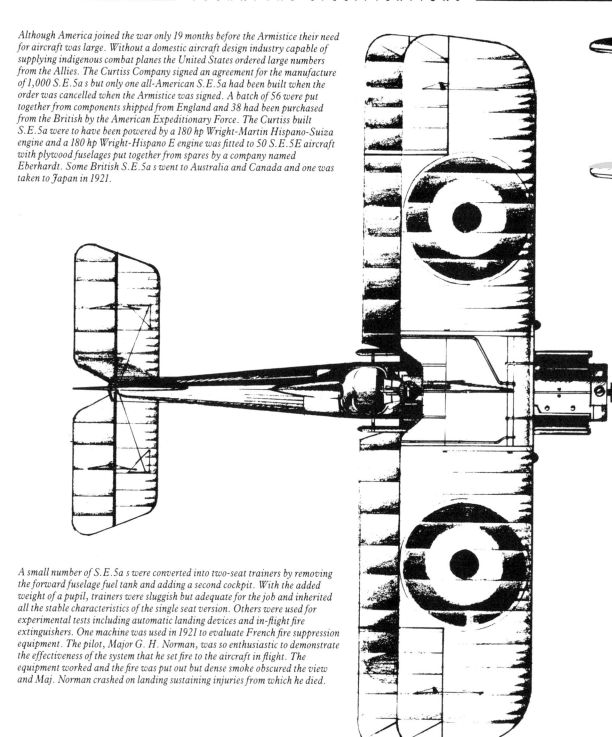

A small number of S.E.5a s were converted into two-seat trainers by removing the forward fuselage fuel tank and adding a second cockpit. With the added weight of a pupil, trainers were sluggish but adequate for the job and inherited all the stable characteristics of the single seat version. Others were used for experimental tests including automatic landing devices and in-flight fire extinguishers. One machine was used in 1921 to evaluate French fire suppression equipment. The pilot, Major G. H. Norman, was so enthusiastic to demonstrate the effectiveness of the system that he set fire to the aircraft in flight. The equipment worked and the fire was put out but dense smoke obscured the view and Maj. Norman crashed on landing sustaining injuries from which he died.

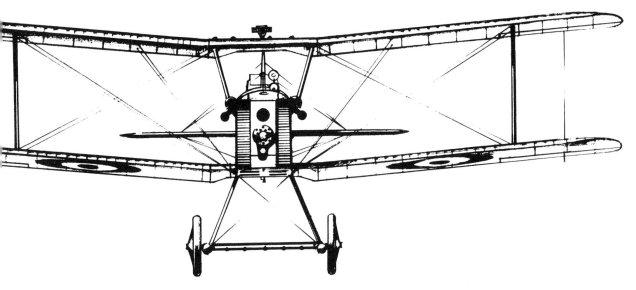

Had the S.E.5a been introduced earlier it would undoubtedly have had a greater impact on the air war than it did. Nevertheless, several leading air aces found it an admirable mount for their endeavours and fought in it with success. Although less agile than the, albeit temperamental, Sopwith Camel the S.E.5a was strong and could be pushed hard in the air. Its ability to absorb damage and take rough treatment endeared it to many who saw in the S.E.5a a culmination of three years of air combat design experience. The precursor S.E.5 powered by the 150 hp Hispano-Suiza is depicted in the side-view on page 123 while the three-view on these pages shows the S.E.5a with a Wolsely Viper engine and with the wooden undercarriage legs fitted to late models.

Overleaf

One of 200 S.E.5a scouts ordered from Vickers Ltd on July 19, 1918, F8963 displays all the many admirable aspects of this rugged and successful design. This particular aircraft was in a batch bearing the serials F8946-F9145 and served with No. 85 Squadron, RFC. Clearly seen is the Foster mounting for the overwing Lewis gun and the single Vickers gun. Early Foster mountings typified by the design used with the Nieuport 17 (see colour three-view on pages 72-73) had restricted movement down and back toward the pilot. This hindered access to the ammunition drum on top. Later Foster mountings had an extended lower section permitting the pilot to pull the gun further back down toward the cockpit. This modified type was fitted to all late production aircraft.

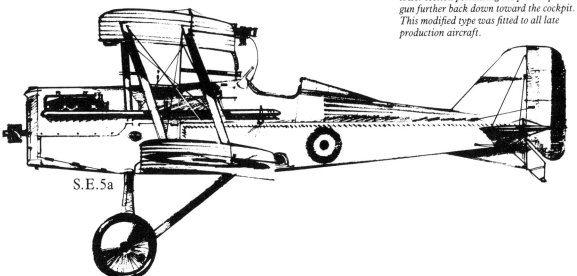

S.E.5a